BEFORE
COLUMBUS

CHARLES C. MANN

COLU

FORE
MBUS

THE AMERICAS OF 1491

A DOWNTOWN BOOKWORKS BOOK • ATHENEUM BOOKS FOR YOUNG READERS • NEW YORK LONDON TORONTO SYDNEY

Atheneum Books for Young Readers
An imprint of Simon & Schuster Children's Publishing Division
1230 Avenue of the Americas
New York, New York 10020

Copyright © 2009 by Charles C. Mann and Downtown Bookworks Inc.

Atheneum Books for Young Readers is a registered trademark of Simon & Schuster, Inc.
For information about special discounts for bulk purchases, please contact
Simon & Schuster Special Sales at 1-866-506-1949 or business@simonandschuster.com.
The Simon & Schuster Speakers Bureau can bring authors to your live event. For more
information or to book an event, contact the Simon & Schuster Speakers Bureau at
1-866-248-3049 or visit our website at www.simonspeakers.com.

Book design by Red Herring
The text of this book was set in Hoefler.

Manufactured in China

10 9 8 7 6 5 4 3 2

Library of Congress Cataloging-in-Publication Data
Mann, Charles C.
Before Columbus : the Americas of 1491 / Charles C. Mann ; [adapted by] Rebecca Stefoff. — 1st ed.
p.   cm. — (A downtown bookworks book)
ISBN: 978-1-4169-4900-8
1. Indians—Origin—Juvenile literature. 2. Indians—History—Juvenile literature.
3. Indians—Antiquities—Juvenile literature. 4. America—Antiquities—Juvenile literature.
I. Mann, Charles C. 1491. II. Title.
E61.S87 2009
970.01—dc22   2009007691
1009 SCP

CONTENTS

ONE OF MY ANCESTORS WAS JOHN BILLINGTON. HE CAME TO THE Americas with the Pilgrims, one of the 102 English people who sailed on the *Mayflower* to the coast of Massachusetts in November 1620. I heard the story of the Pilgrims many times from my grandparents and teachers before I realized that the Pilgrims had shown up in New England without food or shelter six weeks before winter. Despite this unbelievable lack of preparation, half of them managed not to die in the ice and snow. (Fortunately for me, Billington was one of them.) To me, this was amazing. How had *any* of the Pilgrims survived?

My school history book gave an answer. "A friendly Indian named Squanto helped the colonists," it said. "He showed them how to plant corn and how to live on the edge of the wilderness." Years later, I found out that the true name of that Indian was Tisquantum. I also learned that the real story of how he helped the Pilgrims was more complicated than the version in my history book. It was more interesting, too.

The Pilgrims were flabbergasted to discover that Tisquantum already spoke English. He did so because six years earlier some visiting European sailors had kidnapped him and sold him into slavery in Spain. (At the time, slavery was common in parts of Europe.) A group of antislavery priests rescued Tisquantum. Trying to escape, he somehow got to England, where he was put up by a British merchant, who probably viewed him as a living museum exhibit. At the merchant's house, Tisquantum learned English and talked his way onto a boat sailing for America.

Tisquantum belonged to the Wampanoag alliance, a group of Native American villages in what is now Massachusetts and Rhode Island. Just as I learned in my history book, the Wampanoag leader asked Tisquantum to live with and help the Pilgrims. Historians now know, however, that Tisquantum agreed to do it partly because he wanted to get the Pilgrims on his side. If they attacked his enemies, he could become the most powerful person in Wampanoag society. In the end, Tisquantum's plan failed, but he almost started a civil war.

The Pilgrims had a hard time understanding Tisquantum's plots. Misled by their own preconceptions and beliefs, they had a terrible time understanding Indians at all.

Opposite: The arrival of the Pilgrims in Massachusetts

(The Indians, too, had trouble understanding the Pilgrims.) Eventually, the two very different societies—Pilgrim and Wampanoag—ended up fighting a bloody, brutal war. The Pilgrims won the war. Even so, they never really knew *why* they won. It wasn't until the 1960s—hundreds of years after my ancestor Billington landed—that historians fully grasped why small groups of poorly prepared European colonists were able to defeat much bigger Indian societies.

Why did the Europeans win? The Pilgrims had little in the way of weapons, and they didn't know how to survive in this new land. Why weren't *they* wiped out? Was it because there were simply too few Native Americans to withstand the flood of migrants from Europe? Was it because Indian societies had too little technology? Or was there some other reason?

Above: A Native American watches the Pilgrims come ashore from the *Mayflower*. The meeting between Europeans and Indians would bring surprises for both.

That's one thing I wanted to find out when I started writing the adult version of this book, *1491*. The answer, which involved events that happened thousands of years ago, surprised me. It's the subject of Part Two of this book.

Part One is about another, more basic question. When Europeans first came to the Americas, they often described the land as "lightly settled." It was as if Indians had lived there for thousands of years and hadn't built anything. How, I wondered, could that possibly be true? People everywhere else in the world created farms, made scientific discoveries, and built great cities. After college, I lived in Italy for two years. When I drove around the countryside, it was full of signs of the past—Roman ruins, Renaissance churches, Etruscan walls. Was there nothing like these great early civilizations in the Americas? Was the New World, as Europeans called it, really so new?

That question is linked to a third question. Today, the environmental laws in the United States are designed to bring the country's rivers, fields, and forests back to the way they were when only Indians lived in the Americas. Before my ancestor Billington arrived, my history books told me, this whole half of the world was basically a wilderness: an empty landscape, nature in the raw. Again I wondered, could that possibly be true? Did Indians live here for so long and leave the land almost untouched? Part Three of this book looks at that question.

When I was in school in the 1970s my history books told me the answers to those questions. Now, however, many researchers think that almost everything I was taught about early American history was wrong, especially the parts about Native Americans. A whole new picture is forming: It shows what life was like in the Americas before Christopher Columbus arrived in 1492, and it also shows how the arrival of Europeans affected the Americas.

Native Americans created societies that were older, bigger, and more highly developed than we used to think. They left their mark on the land in ways that may surprise you. As I found out—and as you'll see in the following pages—dozens of new discoveries and ideas are giving us a better, clearer, and very different picture of the Americas before Columbus than the one I was taught in school. It's a picture I bet my ancestor Billington would have liked to have learned about.

Native America, AD 1492

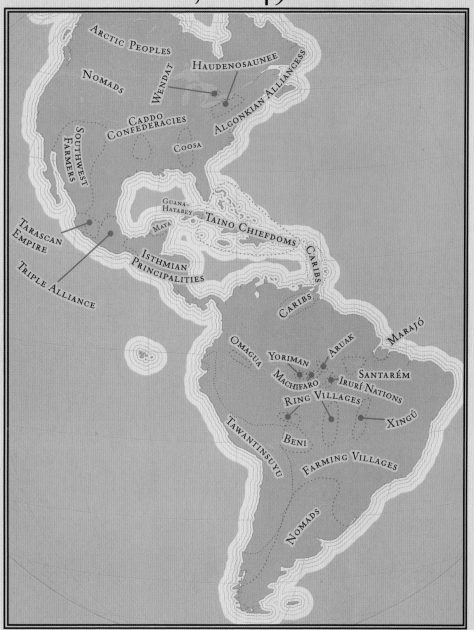

Arctic Peoples

Nomads

Wendat

Haudenosaunee

Algonkian Alliances

Caddo Confederacies

Coosa

Southwest Farmers

Guana-Hatabey

Taino Chiefdoms

Maya

Caribs

Tarascan Empire

Isthmian Principalities

Triple Alliance

Caribs

Omagua

Yoriman

Aruak

Marajó

Machifaro

Santarém

Irurí Nations

Ring Villages

Xingú

Tawantinsuyu

Beni

Farming Villages

Nomads

PART ONE
HOW OLD WAS THE "NEW WORLD"?

WHEN EUROPEANS SAILED ACROSS THE ATLANTIC Ocean in the late fifteenth century, they found lands that they called a "New World." Those lands were the Americas, home to millions of people — and some ancient civilizations.

One center of civilization arose thousands of years ago in the Andes Mountains of South America. Another took shape far to the north in Mesoamerica, which includes most of Mexico and the lands on its southern border. Forests, swamps, and mountains kept the Andean and Meso-american cultures apart, and they were very different from one another. They were also very different from the first societies in Asia, Egypt, and Europe — but they were just about as old. Recent discoveries have shown that civilization in the Americas began earlier than anyone thought.

CHAPTER 1

CITIES
IN THE DESERT

FOR GENERATIONS, HISTORIANS THOUGHT THEY KNEW HOW civilization began. It started when the people of the Middle East invented agriculture about 11,000 years ago. Later, a civilization called Sumer developed in Mesopotamia, now part of Iraq. By about 4000 BC, some Sumerian farming villages were becoming the first cities. Over time, important parts of Sumerian culture, such as farming, city building, and writing, spread to the rest of Mesopotamia and to Egypt and beyond. Everything in Europe could be traced back to its beginnings in Sumer.

Civilization in the Americas, said the historians, began in Mesoamerica, the region that includes Mexico and Central America, about 3,000 or 3,500 years ago. This meant that American civilization began about the time that the first organized states were taking shape in China—but it was much younger than Middle Eastern civilization. At least, that's what the experts thought.

However, since the 1990s, a series of astonishing discoveries on the coast of South America has given us a new view of the birth of American civilization. Five thousand years ago, there were only a handful of cities in the world. The biggest urban center of all might have been a cluster of small cities in the desert of Peru.

Opposite: The ancient Peruvian city of Caral had a large temple, an amphitheater (the round structures behind the temple), and pyramids.

Above: Fog shrouds the Peruvian coast, a cool cloudy strip of land that is one of the Earth's most unusual deserts.

A STRANGE DESERT

The high, rugged Andes Mountains run along the west coast of South America like the bony spine of a continent-sized sleeping dinosaur. Farther west is the Pacific Ocean. Sandwiched between the two is a long, narrow, gray-brown strip of desert. This dry region is the coast of Peru.

To the south, the desert stretches into the coast of Chile, Peru's neighbor. There, it is called the Atacama Desert, and it is the driest place on Earth. In some parts of this desert, rain has never been known to fall. When space scientists need a place that's as much like the sands of Mars as possible, they go to the Atacama.

Peru's coastal desert is not quite as dry as the Atacama. It gets about two inches (five centimeters) of water each year, mostly in the form of fog. On winter mornings, the cold ocean air along the coast fills with moist fog banks that roll into the valleys and linger for hours before they melt away.

The coast of Peru is not a desert like the Sahara, though, with sand dunes and scorching sun. More than 50 rivers plunge down from the Andes, cutting through the coastal desert on their way to the Pacific. Lined with vegetation, these rivers are long, green oases in the almost lifeless land.

Archaeologists, who study ancient people and civilizations, have recently found traces of some of the first people to live in Peru's coastal desert. These early inhabitants dug up wedge clams and chased schools of six-inch drumfish with nets on the beach then carried the food inland to their base. Signs of their presence on the land date from before 10,000 BC or 12,000 years ago.

Right: People of the Chinchorro culture developed elaborate methods of mummification as early as 6000 BC.

THE MUMMY MAKERS

By 8000 BC people lived throughout western South America. Modern historians call these early Americans Paleoindians, from the Greek word *paleo*, which means "old." Some Paleoindians lived on the coast of Peru, as their ancestors had done, weaving nets to catch fish. Others plucked fish from mangrove swamps or settled into mountain caves and lived by skewering deer-sized animals called *vicuña* on spears.

We know very little about the beliefs and customs of these early people. Archaeologists must try to piece together a picture from the things they left behind—such as the world's first mummies.

The Chinchorro people lived in the Atacama Desert. Sometime before 5000 BC, they began to mummify the bodies of children and, later, adults. The process was somewhat gruesome. They peeled off the skin of the dead like a sock. Then they covered the body with white clay and painted it to look like the dead person. As a last touch, they gave each mummy a wig made of his or her own hair. These mummies were repainted often, which probably means that they were kept on display, perhaps for years.

Nobody knows what made the Chinchorro begin to mummify their dead, but the practice is the first sign of a belief that other Indian civilizations around the Andes Mountains would later share. All of them honored and preserved their dead.

TROUBLE WITH TAPEWORMS

The skill of the ancient Chinchorro mummy makers, together with the dry climate of the Atacama Desert, preserved the dead bodies so well that modern scientists have been able to get DNA from them. Scientists investigating the mummies have discovered that the Chinchorro were infected by parasites from raw seafood. These marine tapeworms attach themselves to a person's intestines and can grow to lengths of 16 feet. Their victims get sick and eventually die. No wonder some of the child mummies of the Chinchorro show signs of fatal illness!

Norte Chico
The Americas' First Urban Complex, 3000–1800 BC

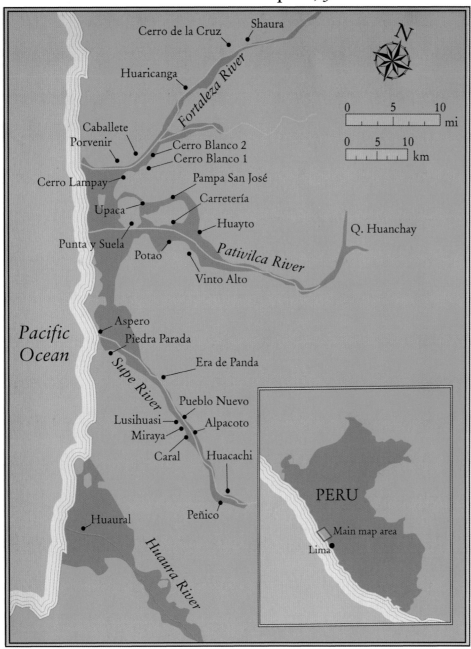

THE SURPRISING CITIES OF THE NORTE CHICO

North of Lima, the capital city of Peru, lies a part of the coastal desert known as the Norte Chico. It is made up of four river valleys. At the bottom of each valley, a river lined with greenery winds toward the coast.

The Norte Chico is dotted with large mounds of earth. For years, some people thought these mounds might hold ancient ruins. Then, in 1941, a pair of American archaeologists made the first serious study of the Norte Chico. They excavated, or dug into, a place called Aspero, in a salt marsh at the mouth of one of the rivers.

The archaeologists discovered a big trash heap and an ancient building with many rooms. They found no pottery, though, and only a few cobs of Indian corn, or maize. This was a puzzle because maize was supposed to be the Indians' main food. Why were there so few traces of it at Aspero? How had the Indians grown maize in a salt marsh, anyway?

The age of the Aspero site was a mystery, too. In the 1950s, scientists began to develop a tool called radiocarbon dating. It measures how much time has passed since the death of anything that was once alive. Archaeologists could use this new technology to find the age of bone, wood, cloth, leather, and other things containing plant or animal tissue.

Not until the 1970s was radiocarbon dating used at Aspero. An archaeology student doing new research there was able to afford some tests. The results surprised him. One of the tests gave the area a date of 3000 BC.

"Ridiculous," the student thought. The structures at Aspero were too big to be that old. It would mean that the people who lived in Peru were building big pyramids before the Egyptians—and that would turn history on its head. The student was sure that something had gone wrong with the tests.

The next surprise came in 1994, when a Peruvian archaeologist started working on a site called Caral, inland from Aspero. She uncovered 150 acres of structures, including big stone buildings with apartments. There were also many platforms made of earth that had been piled and packed down. One platform was 60 feet tall and 500 feet long. Caral, it was clear, had once been a major settlement—but how old was it?

Radiocarbon dating showed that Caral was founded before 2600 BC. The history books would have to be rewritten. Caral's platforms and buildings had been identified as the oldest known city in the Americas.

This situation was short lived, however. In 2004, a team of archaeologists reported the ages of sites they had explored along the Fortaleza River, in the northern part of the Norte Chico, in Peru. Several of these sites were older than Caral. One with pyramids, Huaricanga, dates from about 3500 BC. It is currently the oldest known American city.

Radiocarbon dating showed that Caral was founded before 2600 BC. The history books would have to be rewritten.

Above: This amphitheater forms a part of an elaborate urban complex in the ancient city of Caral.

A NEW BIRTHPLACE OF CIVILIZATION

For generations before the discovery of Caral, Huaricanga, and the other Norte Chico cities, historians believed that the first American civilization, or advanced way of life, arose in Mesoamerica, the region that includes Mexico and Central America. The idea was that ancient Mesoamericans must have visited Peru, and the Peruvians must have borrowed skills, customs, and beliefs from them. But Huaricanga dates from 3500 BC, which made it *older* than any Mesoamerican culture. This proved that civilization arose independently in Peru.

During the 1,000 years after the founding of Huaricanga, the people of the Norte Chico built more cities. Archaeologists have discovered about 25 of them so far. None of them was close to the size of cities in Sumer, the birthplace of civilization in the Middle East, but taken all together, they were bigger than Sumer. Huaricanga and at least six other early Norte Chico cities had large public buildings—including pyramid-like structures that may have been used for religious ceremonies—centuries before the Egyptians. When the people of the Norte Chico were building their cities, Sumer was the only other urban center on earth.

One mound at Huaricanga looked like a big sandhill. When the archaeologists started to excavate it, they found, beneath a layer of earth, stone walls that had once been smoothly plastered. They cleared the top of a huge platform and stairs leading up to it. Soon they could see enough of the structure to map its outline. It was 150 feet long and 60 feet high, in the shape of a huge U, with a sunken plaza between the two arms. When this structure was under construction, it was among the biggest buildings in the world.

Archaeologists call the big mound at Huaricanga—and those like it in other Norte Chico sites—temples because they were most likely built for religious reasons. Its size and grandeur would have overwhelmed everyone who saw it. It is certain that constructing this temple took a lot of work. People don't often volunteer to spend their days carrying baskets of heavy rocks to build public monuments, however. Planning and controlling that kind of work takes leaders who have power or influence over others. That's why archaeologists who are studying Huaricanga and other nearby ruins say that the Norte Chico was the second place in the world, after Mesopotamia, where centralized governments appeared.

COTTON BOLLS AND LITTLE FISH

No burned buildings, mutilated corpses, or other signs of war have been found in the Norte Chico. The cities there were not built for protection, or as forts. Instead, they were probably places of worship and perhaps of trade. What did the people of Norte Chico have to trade, though? How did they live?

In Sumer, Egypt, India, and China, civilization began with the large-scale farming of food crops. Fields of grain fed the growing populations and made civilization possible. Previously, archaeologists and historians thought that all civilizations started that way.

By digging miles and miles of irrigation ditches, the inhabitants of Norte Chico made their land fertile.

Now some of them think that Andean civilization was based on something completely different: fishing.

The early Paleoindian inhabitants of the Norte Chico got most of their food from the sea, not the land. The ruins of Aspero and other coastal sites contain a lot of fishbones but almost no evidence of food crops. Some researchers suspect that the oldest settlements in the Norte Chico were the coastal fishing communities. Only later did people move inland and take up farming, and when they did turn to agriculture, their main crop was not food, but cotton for fishing nets.

Dry as it is, the Norte Chico is well suited for irrigation. The land is steep, and the rivers that carry snowmelt from the Andes shoot quickly toward the sea. The people who lived there thousands of years ago found that if they dug channels to carry water from the rivers out into the landscape, it flowed through the channels swiftly enough that it did not evaporate, leaving salts and minerals behind. This meant that the people could irrigate their fields and grow crops for centuries without poisoning the soil with built-up chemicals. By digging miles and miles of irrigation ditches, the inhabitants of the Norte Chico made their land fertile.

They used that fertile land to grow cotton, which once grew wild along the coasts of South America. The local cotton plant produced fibers in long, puffy pods called bolls. The people of Norte Chico learned to weave the cotton fibers into thread and cloth. There are no statues or carvings in the ancient buildings of the Norte Chico, but there are some pieces of woven cloth.

Cotton was part of a regional trade network between the coast and the inland towns. People in Huaricanga, Caral, and other inland towns grew cotton, along with fruits and vegetables, in their irrigated fields. People in Aspero and other shoreline settlements caught vast quantities of fish, especially anchovies and sardines, small fish that thrive in the cold currents off Peru's coast. In return for providing fish to the people in the inland towns, the coastal people got the cotton they needed for their nets.

Was civilization in Peru truly based on fishing, not farming? That is one of many questions that can be answered only by more research in the Norte Chico. Already, though, this long-neglected patch of Peruvian coastline is giving historians a new view of the ancient American past. Norte Chico lighted a cultural fire. Over the next 3,000 years, many cultures would rise and fall in Peru. With its large public construction projects, its trade, and its use of cotton and textiles, Norte Chico may have set a pattern for all of them.

THE CASE OF THE CARVED GOURD

Archaeologists love artifacts. These man-made objects may be tools, pieces of pottery, golden crowns, or simple household utensils such as wooden spoons, but each one has a story to tell. Like the buildings left behind by vanished cultures, artifacts are clues to how people lived—even, sometimes, what they believed.

A carved gourd may be the only surviving trace of the Norte Chico people's gods. The gourd was found in a valley south of Huaricanga, in what seems to be an ancient cemetery. Cut into the surface of the dried gourd is a picture of a sharp-toothed figure. He wears a hat and holds a staff, or pole, in each hand. Some researchers think this is the oldest known image of the Staff God, who appears in the art and religion of the later cultures of the Andes Mountains, all the way up to the Inca people of modern times. If this is true, the Staff God, a major part of the Andean religious tradition, originated in Norte Chico, and the tradition remained unbroken for 4,000 years.

A big question hangs over the age of the carving, however. Radiocarbon tests show that the gourd was harvested around 2200 BC. When the archaeologists found it, though, it was in a layer of material from thousands of years later, between AD 900 and 1300. Does this mean that people treasured and preserved the ancient carved gourd for 3,000 years? Or does it mean that someone who lived around the year AD 1000 came across a 3,000-year-old dried gourd one day and decided to carve a picture of the Staff God into it? The case of the carved gourd reminds us that even when we find artifacts from the distant past, we cannot always discover exactly what they mean.

Pativilca Valley,
Norte Chico

2280–2180 BC

Karwa,
Chavin

500–300 BC

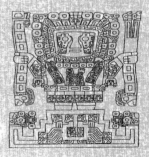

Gateway of the Sun,
Tiwanaku

300–1000 AD

CHAPTER 2

GENETIC
ENGINEERING

IF YOU ASKED MODERN SCIENTISTS TO name the world's greatest achievements in genetic engineering, you might be surprised by one of their low-tech answers: maize.

Scientists know that maize, called "corn" in the United States, was created more than 6,000 years ago. Although exactly how this well-known plant was invented is still a mystery, they do know where it was invented—in the narrow "waist" of southern Mexico. This jumble of mountains, beaches, wet tropical forests, and dry plains is the most ecologically diverse part of Mesoamerica. Today, it is home to more than a dozen different Indian groups, but the human history of these hills and valleys stretches far into the past.

FROM HUNTING TO GATHERING TO FARMING

About 11,500 years ago a group of Paleoindians was living in caves in what is now the Mexican state of Puebla. These people were hunters, but they did not bring down mastodons and mammoths. Those huge species were already extinct. Instead, the hunters preyed on smaller game, such as deer and jackrabbits. Now and then they even feasted on giant turtles (which were probably a lot easier to catch than the fast-moving deer and rabbits).

Over the next 2,000 years, though, game animals grew scarce. Maybe the people of the area had been too successful at hunting. Maybe, as the climate grew slowly hotter and drier, the grasslands where the animals lived shrank, and so the animal populations shrank, as well. Perhaps the situation was a combination of these two reasons. Whatever the explanation, hunters of Puebla and the neighboring state of Oaxaca turned to plants for more of their food.

Opposite: Some of the many different varieties of maize
still grown in southern Mexico

Their lives—and their diets—were shaped by the rhythm of the seasons. For most of the year, individual families lived by themselves, moving from place to place. During the winter, they hunted. In spring and fall, they gathered seeds and fruits. By summer, one of their favorite foods—cactus leaves—was plentiful enough to feed larger groups. With enough food available, 25 or 30 people might gather in a band to spend the season together.

Meanwhile, the people kept learning about their environment. They discovered that the thick-leaved, cactus-like agave plants could be eaten if they were first roasted over a fire. They found a way to make acorns into nutritious food: grind them into powder, then soak the powder in water and let it dry. Along the way, people might have noticed that seeds they threw into the garbage one year would sprout as new plants the next year. At some point, they started to intentionally scatter seeds, so that they would have food to gather during the next growing season. They were practicing agriculture.

This happened in many places across southern Mexico. People began to grow food crops that are still harvested across Mesoamerica today—squash, gourds, and peppers. Then came maize.

THE MYSTERY OF MAIZE

If when you think of corn, you see yellow kernels, Mexican maize might surprise you. It can be red, blue, yellow, orange, black, pink, purple, creamy white, and even multicolored. People in one valley may grow cobs the size of a baby's hand, with little red kernels no bigger than grains of rice that turn into tiny puffs when they are popped.

In the next valley, maize plants produce two-foot-long cobs, with big fluffy kernels that people float in their soup.

Maize is a cereal, like wheat, rice, barley, and many other grains, but it looks and acts differently from the rest. Other cereals can reproduce themselves by scattering their grains. Maize kernels, which are the plant's seeds, are wrapped in a tough husk and don't scatter naturally. This means that maize can't reproduce on its own—it has to be planted by people. Other cereals grew wild before people began to farm them,

No wild ancestor of maize has ever been found.

and in many places they still grow wild today. No wild ancestor of maize has ever been found, however. So where did it come from?

In the 1960s, an archaeological team combed the Tehuacán Valley in Puebla, Central Mexico, for signs of early agriculture. The archaeologists sifted through 49 caves before they found anything. In the fiftieth site, they found ancient maize cobs no bigger than a small toe.

All in all, the team found more than 23,000 whole or broken maize cobs in the valley. These little cobs became the ammunition in a debate about the origins of maize. One side thought that maize must have come from a wild ancestor plant that is now extinct. This vanished plant interbred long ago with other wild grasses, and the result was maize.

The other side in the debate claimed that maize was descended from its closest known relative, teosinte, a kind of wild mountain grass. Teosinte looks nothing like maize, though, and it is not a practical food source. Its hard, woody seeds are sparse. A whole ear of teosinte has less nutritional value than a single kernel of maize. Plant scientists couldn't explain how teosinte might have evolved naturally into maize.

But some experts think maize came from a mutated form of teosinte. Mutations occur naturally in nature, when the genetic codes of parent plants or animals get slightly scrambled in their offspring. The Indians might have noticed that a mutated form of teosinte seemed a little more useful. They could have picked through stands of teosinte, looking for the plants with the useful qualities, then bred them with each other to create a new generation of plants. Experts think that skilled, determined plant breeders could have turned the right teosinte mutations into maize in just ten years.

Maybe teosinte is not the answer. Another idea about the origin of maize is that Indians came across a hybrid cereal plant that had come about by chance when two different kinds of wild grasses hybridized, or crossbred. The Indians realized that they could purposely mix two kinds of grasses by fertilizing one kind with pollen from the other kind. In this way, they could create something new: maize.

To historians, it doesn't really matter whether maize came from teosinte or from other grasses. The key thing is that maize was created by the Indians in a bold act of biological manipulation. The result was a hardy, nutritious new food source that would change agriculture—and society—in Mesoamerica and beyond.

Above: On the left is a wild grass called teosinte, the cob of which is less than two inches long. On the right is a maize cob produced by crossing teosinte with a type of modern South American maize. It looks a lot like the oldest known maize cobs and may offer a clue as to how people created maize.

MAIZE WAS CREATED BY THE INDIANS IN A **BOLD ACT** OF BIOLOGICAL MANIPULATION.

MAGICAL *MILPA*

The Indians of Mesoamerica did more than invent maize. They also perfected the ideal way of growing it. They created the *milpa*, a system of agriculture that has been in use in Mesoamerica for thousands of years.

The word *milpa* means "maize field," but its true meaning is more complex. A *milpa* is a field in which farmers plant many different crops at the same time. In addition to maize, a *milpa* often contains several kinds of beans and squash, avocados, sweet potatoes, tomatoes, chili peppers, melons, and more.

In nature, wild beans can grow next to teosinte. When this happens, the beans benefit because they can use the tall teosinte stalks to climb toward the sun. The teosinte benefits because the beans' roots add nutrients to the soil. Indians either invented this arrangement on their own or adopted it after seeing it in the wild. They put corn and beans together in their *milpa* and added even more plants.

A *milpa* is the beginning of a well-balanced diet. A person who ate only maize would be unhealthy because maize doesn't have two amino acids that the human body needs. Those acids are found in beans, but beans lack another acid, called methionine, that maize just happens to have. Together, though, beans and maize make a complete meal. You could live for a pretty long time on just those two foods, but after a while, your body would miss the vitamins and healthy fats that come from other *milpa* crops, such as squash and avocados.

Below: Wheeled jaguar from Veracruz, Mexico

WHY NO WHEELS?

When the Europeans arrived in the Americas, the Indians had no wheeled vehicles. No carts, wagons, chariots, or wheelbarrows. They did not even have wheels for grinding grain or making pottery, as some other cultures did.

At several places in Mexico, though, archaeologists have found toy-sized figurines, such as dogs and jaguars, with wheels. If the Mesoamericans equipped their toys or models with wheels, why didn't they make bigger wheels and use them on wagons?

Maybe they did not have livestock to pull wagons. There were no domestic horses or cattle in the Americas until the Europeans introduced them. Even with animals, people in wet, heavily forested, and mountainous areas might not have had much use for wheels, because wagons could not travel easily over the ground.

A better reason is simply that even complex societies do not always invent every possible kind of complex technology. The lack of a particular piece of technology doesn't make a civilization inferior. Millions of Europeans, for example, plowed their fields with a painfully inefficient plow for centuries after the Chinese had come up with a much better design. One culture's achievement may be another culture's blind spot.

17

Growing different kinds of plants together is much better than growing a single crop.

The *milpa* has been called one of the most successful of all human inventions, and not just because it is nutritious. The *milpa* can also let people farm the land without wearing out the soil. Today, farmers in Europe and Asia usually plant just one crop in a field. This can drain the soil of nutrients, so the farmers have to add fertilizer, which may bring new problems. This method is expensive, and fertilizer that runs off fields in rainwater may end up in streams, rivers, or the ocean, where it causes an excess growth of the tiny plants known as algae, unbalancing the ecosystem.

Most crops drain the soil of nitrogen, which must be replaced with fertilizer. The *milpa*'s beans, however, put nitrogen into the soil. In addition, by growing multiple crops at the same time, *milpa* farmers imitate the variety found in natural ecosystems. Growing different kinds of plants together is, from an environmental point of view, often much better than growing a single crop. It protects the soil from erosion and nourishes the helpful bacteria and other microorganisms in the soil. The *milpa* is the only known system of farming that has kept some fields productive for more than 4,000 years of constant use. By studying traditional *milpa* farming, agricultural scientists may learn techniques that will help modern industrial farmers preserve the health of their soils.

LANDSCAPES OF FOOD

Before people in the ancient Middle East began to farm wheat, they gathered the grain from wild wheat. Cereal grasses grew naturally across large stretches of the land. People knew what it was like to stand in a field of wheat stretching to the horizon. People in Mesoamerica had never encountered fields of wild grain, though. When the Mesoamericans invented maize, they also invented the grain field for themselves. This landscape of food was completely new in the Americas. This may be why maize played such an important role in many Native American religions. It was not something the Indians took for granted.

MAIZE AROUND THE WORLD

Maize, the product of Native American genetic engineering, was carried to other parts of the world by Europeans after the fifteenth century. Maize quickly became an important food in places where nothing like it had ever grown before.

People in many parts of Europe adopted maize as a staple grain. Unfortunately, they didn't know how to combine maize and beans in a nutritionally complete diet as the Mesoamericans did. Europeans in some regions ate so much maize that they suffered from pellagra. This disease is caused by a lack of niacin (vitamin B3). Maize has niacin, but it is bound up in compounds that the body can't digest unless it has been treated with a type of chemical called an alkali. When Mesoamericans make tortillas, they soak the maize in lime, which makes the niacin in the maize useable by the body. Europeans, however, did not know how to make tortillas.

In Africa, maize became part of a complex web of interconnections. Europeans introduced American maize to Africa, and by the end of the sixteenth century, Africans were raising maize as well as other American foods, including peanuts and manioc. These new crops boosted Africa's food production, leading to a population boom just at the time the Europeans were taking millions of Africans as slaves for their mines and plantations in the Americas. In this way, maize, the foundation of Mesoamerican civilization, may have fed the terrible slave trade.

Left: A Huichol farmer harvests maize in the Sierra Madre Occidental Mountains in Mexico.

Maize and the *milpa* slowly spread beyond their birthplace in Mesoamerica. To the south, maize traveled all the way to Peru and Chile in South America. The people of these Andean lands had developed their own agriculture based on potatoes, but still they prized maize as a luxury item. (Maize didn't seem to catch on in the Amazon basin, though. Most researchers think that manioc, or cassava, as it is sometimes called, was already the staple food there.)

Maize traveled north, too. By the time the Pilgrims came to New England in the seventeenth century, the coast was lined with fields of mixed maize, beans, and squash. In some places, the fields stretched for miles inland from the coast.

First, though, maize conquered Mesoamerica. Archaeologists have found signs that people in southern Mexico were clearing large areas of land for *milpa* as long ago as 2000 to 1500 BC. Maize was part of a great explosion of creativity that took place in Mesoamerica at that time.

Below: A carving of the Maya corn god from AD 500

Great civilizations were about to rise in Mesoamerica. Maize would feed the growing populations that built big new urban centers. It would nourish workers, soldiers, and priests. In their monuments and artworks, the people of these civilizations would honor maize. Stone carvings would show ears of maize springing from the skulls of the gods and decorating the headdresses of kings. One civilization, the Maya, would even say that human beings were created from maize.

CHAPTER 3

FROM OLMEC TO MAYA

ONE DAY IN THE MIDDLE OF THE nineteenth century, a man was walking through the forest near his village in southern Mexico when he stumbled over something in the ground. It was the top of a huge, stone head, sunk to the eyebrows in mud. Eighty years later, that head became the first clue to a forgotten civilization.

THE BIG STONE HEAD

The villager's find sounded important, but the stone head was so big and heavy that no one had the resources to pull it out of the ground. In 1938, an American archaeologist named Matthew W. Stirling went to Veracruz, the Mexican state where the buried head had been found. He wanted to see it for himself.

Veracruz lies on the Gulf of Mexico in southern Mexico. To reach the head, Stirling had to make an

Above: The Olmec sculpture found in Tres Zapotes, Mexico

Tres Zapotes was centuries older than any other Mayan site!

eight-hour horseback ride through the wet, buggy forest to the small village of Tres Zapotes. When he finally found the head, he saw with excitement that it was surrounded by about 50 large man-made mounds of earth. Stirling thought that the mounds, like the head, must have been made by the Maya, who were believed to have created Mesoamerica's first civilization—a society that reached its height about AD 800. Adding to Stirling's excitement was the fact that Tres Zapotes was 150 miles west of any known Maya city. Maybe the Maya realm had been bigger than anyone suspected. He decided to come back the next year and explore the site in more detail.

When Stirling returned to Tres Zapotes, he and his team dug the dirt away from the great head. At last they could see its face—deep-set eyes, a flat nose, and broad lips in a stern expression. The head seemed to be wearing a close-fitting helmet. The natural, lifelike appearance of the sculpture was different from the stiff, highly decorated look of most ancient Mesoamerican carvings.

Stirling and his crew also found a stone pillar covered with intricate carved images. Then they found two more pillars in the ground. To Stirling's disappointment, one pillar was blank. The other was so badly weathered that its carvings could not be made out. Stirling asked his crew of villagers to raise that slab so he could see the other side. As the men brushed the dirt from the back of the slab, one cried out in Spanish, "Chief! Here are numbers!"

The men had discovered clusters of the carved bars and dots that the Maya used for writing numbers. The numbers on the slab formed a date, one that translated to September 3, 32 BC. This meant that the carvings on the stone were more than 1,900 years old. Suddenly, Stirling faced the fact that Tres Zapotes was not just outside Maya territory—it was centuries older than any other Maya site was thought to be!

As Stirling saw it, there were two possibilities. One was that the Maya had originated earlier and farther west than anyone thought, and then simply moved their whole culture eastward. That didn't seem very likely. The other possibility, that Tres Zapotes was not a Maya settlement, didn't seem likely, either. Everyone knew that the Maya were Meso-america's oldest advanced society. Who else could have carved the head and the pillars?

LA VENTA

Local people told Stirling of many other mound sites in Veracruz. He came back in 1940, determined to survey them all. The task was a challenge, even for an adventurer like Stirling. He had to trek deep into trackless mangrove swamps and travel up narrow, unmapped rivers choked with weeds. Mosquitoes were a constant torment, but the ticks were worse. Stirling had to dig the plentiful insects out of his flesh with the point of a knife.

One site Stirling examined was La Venta. Although it was in the middle of a coastal swamp, La Venta was dry, raised on an artificial island. There, Stirling's team found four more giant heads, each at least six feet tall and 15 feet around. Carved from a single block of volcanic stone, each head weighed about ten tons. Stirling could not tell how these massive stones had been carried from their source in the distant mountains.

La Venta was filled with mounds, a sign that many people had once lived there. Stirling decided that they could not have been Maya. Their way of life seemed too different from what was known about Maya culture. He decided that the people of La Venta were an unknown culture that had emerged suddenly and mysteriously from the jungle. They were the "mother culture" of the Maya and all the other civilizations that followed in Mesoamerica. Stirling called these mysterious people the Olmec.

Above: Ruins of the Olmec culture in Laguna de los Cerros, Veracruz, Mexico

Mesoamerica, 1000 BC–AD 1000

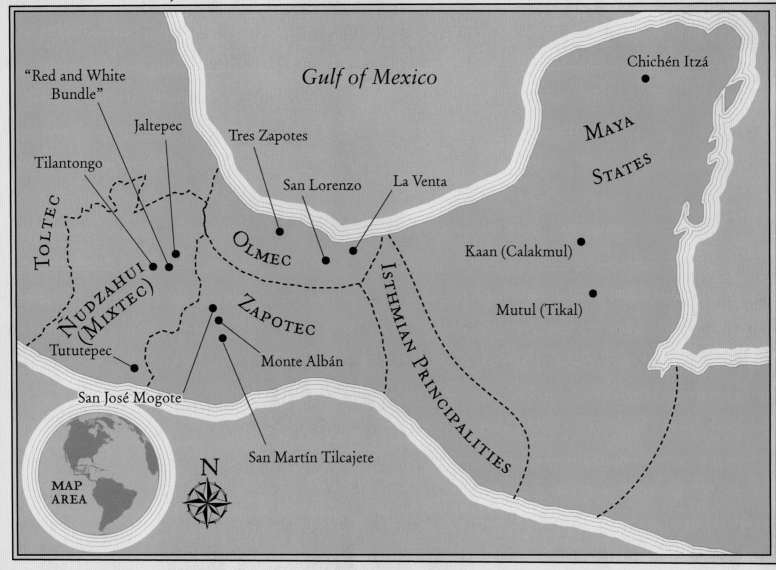

Gulf of Mexico

Chichén Itzá

Maya States

"Red and White Bundle"

Jaltepec

Tres Zapotes

Tilantongo

San Lorenzo

La Venta

Toltec

Olmec

Kaan (Calakmul)

Nudzahui (Mixtec)

Zapotec

Mutul (Tikal)

Isthmian Principalities

Tututepec

Monte Albán

San José Mogote

N

San Martín Tilcajete

MAP AREA

For thousands of years, Mesoamerica was a wellspring of cultural innovation and growth. This map shows some of the most important societies that lived here over a two-thousand-year span.

RUBBER PEOPLE

Nobody knows what the Olmec called themselves, but it wasn't "Olmec." That word comes from Nahuatl, the language of the Mexica people, who lived farther north in Mexico. It means something like "people of the land of rubber." The name fits, though—sort of. In the 1990s, scientists discovered that the Olmec people of La Venta knew how to make rubber from the sap of a tropical tree. They may even have invented rubber.

Archaeologists have learned a lot about the Olmec since Stirling's discoveries. They now know that the Olmec culture formed around 1800 BC in the coastal forests of Veracruz, where farmers planted *milpa* along the rivers. Over the next three centuries, the Olmec built their first great city, San Lorenzo, on a platform made of rocks hauled from mountains 50 miles away. Because the Olmec did not have livestock to haul things for them, people must have done the heavy hauling—though archaeologists are unsure how, exactly, they moved these enormous stones through a swamp. The platform of San Lorenzo was scattered with massive stone thrones for living kings. When a king died, his throne might become the seat for a giant sculpture of his head.

San Lorenzo was destroyed around 900 BC. Maybe the city was invaded by enemies, or maybe the Olmec overthrew their own leaders or smashed their city for religious reasons. By that time, though, they were building a much bigger city about 40 miles away. It was La Venta, and at its center was a huge, bulging clay mound 103 feet tall. It looked something like a gigantic head of garlic.

Researchers don't know why the Olmec built the clay mound or what it meant to them. They do know that La Venta lasted for 800 years. At the height of the city's size and power, elements of Olmec culture spread far and wide throughout Mesoamerica.

LOOKING GOOD AMONG THE OLMEC

In ancient Mesoamerica, if you were a high-ranking or noble Olmec, it wasn't easy being beautiful. Archaeologists think that these people reshaped their newborn babies' heads by strapping small, flat pieces of wood to the infants' skulls. The wood pushed up the soft young bones, creating skulls that were taller than normal. Wealthy Olmec also carved deep grooves in their teeth as a sign of status, and wore plugs of jade through holes pierced in their noses. All of the evidence for these practices comes from Olmec artwork, however, because no Olmec skeletons have ever been found.

MOTHER OR SISTER?

Was Stirling right? Were the Olmec the "mother culture" that set the pattern for all the other "daughter" cultures in the region? Some experts think so. Others have a different idea. They call the Olmec and other Mesoamerican groups "sister cultures."

In the "sister" view, the Olmec arose first, but the cultures that soon followed did not simply follow the Olmec pattern. Instead, all of the cultures influenced each other. As they interacted through trade and war, they borrowed ideas, beliefs, and ways of doing things. Mesoamerica was a cultural stew. The Olmec may have flavored the broth, but other ingredients added their own distinct tastes.

One of these ingredients was the Zapotec, who lived in the central valley of Oaxaca, across the mountains from the Olmec. Their valley was divided into three main chiefdoms. Archaeologists call the biggest one San José Mogote, after a village that now stands near the site. Around 750 BC, archaeologists believe this Zapotec settlement was attacked and its temple burned. The fire raged hot enough to melt the clay walls.

Below: A Mayan calendar column found in the Yucatán Peninsula in Mexico

The people of San José Mogote quickly built a new temple. They placed a sculpture of a bleeding corpse, probably a defeated enemy, right across the threshold, so people could stomp on it as they entered the temple. Two marks were carved between the corpse's feet. They are glyphs, symbols in Mesoamerican writing. If the temple was built around 750 BC and the glyphs were carved at that time, they are the oldest dated writing in the Americas.

COUNTING AND WRITING

Writing begins with counting. In Mesoamerica, the earliest form of counting was keeping track of the date. The Olmec, Zapotec, and Maya were sharp sky watchers. They knew the movements of the moon, planets, and stars, and they used calendars to track and predict these movements.

Amazingly, Mesoamericans used three different calendars. One was a 365-day yearly calendar like the one we use today. Another was a 260-day sacred calendar that might have been based on the orbit of the planet Venus—scientists aren't sure. The third calendar was called the Long Count. It counted every day since a starting point in the year 3114 BC.

Using all three calendars together, as the Mesoamericans did, takes mathematical knowledge. It also requires the idea of zero to fill certain places in calculations. Today we use a number sequence (0 through 9) that was invented by the Hindus and Arabs. The Mesoamericans, though, had invented the zero first. The Long Count, which uses zero, certainly existed by 32 BC, the date on the slab at Tres Zapotes.

How early did the Mesoamericans have calendars? Maybe the carved threshold from San José Mogote holds a hint. The glyphs between the corpse's feet may stand for his name. Some experts think that the glyphs say 1-Earthquake. If that is really the dead man's name, he is the first American to be known to us by name. 1-Earthquake is also a date in the Mesoamerican calendar—which makes sense, because people were often named for their birth dates. So it seems that the Mesoamerican calendar had developed, at least in an early form, by 750 BC.

THE HUNDRED YEARS' WAR

The Zapotec endured for hundreds of years. So did the Mixtec, a collection of small but tough states to the west of Zapotec and Olmec territory. Another group, the Toltec, built an empire to the north, in central Mexico. Finally, in the south rose the culture that was once thought to be the oldest civilization in America: the Maya.

We know now that Maya reached their height between about AD 200 and 900. Then, in one of the great mysteries of archaeology, the heartland of their civilization suddenly collapsed. For years, modern scholars tried to figure out what happened to the Maya. Today, the picture is becoming clearer.

Above: This disemboweled man was found carved in the stone threshold of a temple from 750 BC in San José Mogote. The two symbols between his feet may be the earliest known writing in the Americas.

The heartland of the Maya was the southernmost part of Mexico, where the Yucatán Peninsula juts out into the Gulf of Mexico. By around AD 600, the Maya had turned Yucatán into perhaps the most densely populated place on earth, even though most of the water there is too salty for drinking or irrigation. They managed this by engineering their water supply. They built huge platforms of crushed limestone, paving over the salty swamp bottoms, and they dug reservoirs to hold rainwater, lining them with lime to prevent them from being contaminated by the salty groundwater. The Maya heartland was really a network of artificial "islands" rising out of the landscape.

Although these islands shared a culture, the Maya were not united into a single empire. There were many city-states, each with its own ruler. A few larger city-states dominated the smaller ones. Conflicts between these powerful states could shake Maya society for centuries—and one such struggle helped bring about the fall of the Maya civilization.

Sometime before 561, a ruler known as Sky Witness took the throne of Kaan (now called Calakmul). Sky Witness set out to destroy the larger city-state of Mutal (today known as Tikal). He had a clever plan. He would gain control over all the smaller states surrounding Mutal, causing it to surrender. Things did not go smoothly, however. Mutal fought back.

Under a series of rulers, the war between Kaan and Mutal dragged on for more than a century. The whole region was drawn into the conflict. Half a dozen neighboring cities ended up in ruins. Finally, in 695, Mutal defeated Kaan's army in a bloody battle. Kaan never

A TRAGIC MIXTEC LOVE STORY

The Mixtec recorded their history in documents called codices, painted on deerskin or bark. Most of their codices were later destroyed by the Spanish, but eight survive. Four of them tell the tragic story of a priest-politician named 8-Deer Jaguar Claw.

8-Deer was related to the ruling family of a Mixtec state called Tilantongo. To settle a war with another state, he was sent to a sacred mountain cave, where he met the Priestess of the Dead, a wise and powerful woman who had stripped away the flesh from her jaw, giving her a terrifying, skull-like appearance. The Priestess ordered 8-Deer into exile in a distant town. Not content to rest in exile, 8-Deer put together an army and began to conquer villages and states, building an empire.

Then 8-Deer met and fell in love with 6-Monkey, the young wife of a king who was his greatest enemy. When the two kingdoms went to war, however, 8-Deer's army killed 6-Monkey and her husband. Out of love for 6-Monkey, 8-Deer spared the life of her son—who later raised an army of his own, defeated 8-Deer, disemboweled him, and married his daughter.

recovered from the war's great cost, loss of life, and disruption of trade, but neither did the winner. After another century, Mutal collapsed.

Between AD 800 and 830, cities winked out all over the Mayan heartland. Squatters moved into the great central plazas. The jungle began to reclaim terraces, reservoirs, and mounds. Millions of Maya continued to exist, but the royal governments that had maintained the big urban centers were gone.

Around this time, a terrible drought struck the Yucatán Peninsula. At one time, archaeologists suspected that the drought had wiped out the Mayan cities. The northern part of the Yucatán Peninsula is even drier than the heartland, though, and the Mayan cities there—including the big urban center at Chichén Itzá—survived the drought. In fact, they prospered. Why?

Chichén Itzá may have survived because economic power shifted away from the king to a new class of merchants. The king had directed all trade toward things that proclaimed his glory, such as jewelry for the royal family. The merchants, however, traded salt, chocolate, and cotton harvested in the Yucatán for goods from elsewhere in Mesoamerica that the people needed, such as maize. Chichén Itzá traded its way through the drought.

The Maya had created artificial landscapes that could support big population centers, but only with constant attention. Caught up in visions of glory, the kings in the south had failed to make sure that the fields remained productive and the reservoirs stayed full. If the cities of the Maya heartland had not been pushed to the limit by their long war, would they have survived the drought? That's one question archaeologists might never be able to answer.

Between AD 800 and 830, cities winked out all over the Mayan heartland.

The pyramid of Chichén Itzá in Mexico

CHICHÉN ITZÁ MAY HAVE SURVIVED BECAUSE ECONOMIC POWER SHIFTED AWAY FROM THE KING.

CHAPTER 4

TO THE LAND OF FOUR QUARTERS

WHILE THE SOCIETIES OF MESOAMERICA ROSE AND FELL OVER the centuries, the same thing was happening far to the south, around the ice-capped peaks of the Andes Mountains. Each wave of Andean civilization was bigger and grander than the one before it. The biggest and grandest of all was the Inca empire, founded by a bold prince who shook the world.

A WORLD OF PEAKS AND VALLEYS

On one side of the Andes Mountains is the coastal lowland of western South America. On the other is the huge, forested interior of the continent. In the middle is the long, narrow landscape of the Andean highlands—the only place in the world where people have created a series of advanced, long-lasting civilizations more than 10,000 feet above sea level.

In many places, the Andes Mountains split into two ranges that run side by side. Between them lies a realm of high, windy plains called the altiplano. The ranges themselves are cut by many deep, steep valleys. People who lived in this world of valleys, peaks, and high plains became masters of an uphill–downhill trade network. Each level had something to contribute.

The coast provided fish, cotton, and some corn. In the altiplano, herders tended flocks of grazing animals called llamas and alpacas, sources of meat and wool. The

Opposite: A llama grazing near the ruins of Machu Picchu, the Inca emperor's summer estate, in Peru

Tawantinsuyu
Expansion of the Inca Empire, AD 1438–1527

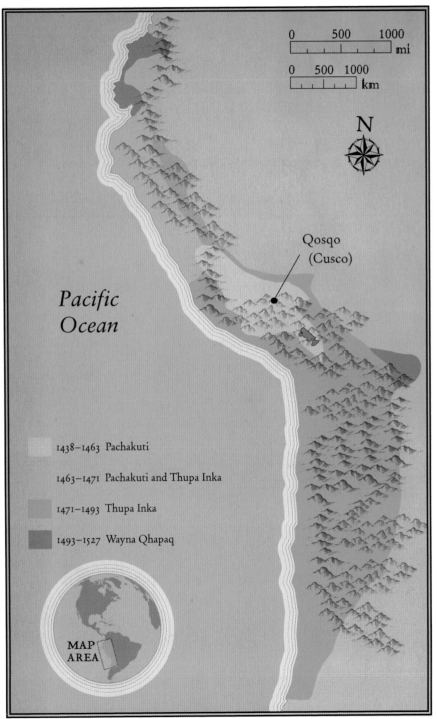

0   500   1000
mi

0   500   1000
km

N

Qosqo
(Cusco)

Pacific
Ocean

1438–1463 Pachakuti

1463–1471 Pachakuti and Thupa Inka

1471–1493 Thupa Inka

1493–1527 Wayna Qhapaq

MAP
AREA

altiplano also produced Peru's many root crops. One of those crops was potatoes, which people freeze-dried and then created a product called *chuño*, which can be made into flour, and, unlike potatoes, can be kept for years. Between the coast and the altiplano, farmers grew beans, squash, and other crops on stone-walled terraces that were carved into the slopes like a million small, flat steps rising one on top of another.

Peru's landscape is so varied that in some places people were able to grow almost everything. Still, by bringing together the products of many different ecosystems, Andean people enjoyed a better life than if they had lived on what was harvested in just one place. They also spread out the risk from natural disasters. A drought, a flood, or an earthquake could destroy crops in one area, but the people could still get food from other parts of their trade network. This economic system supported many societies and kingdoms over the centuries.

WORLDSHAKER

About AD 1200, a small group of people migrated from somewhere in the highlands to a village called Qosqo in the mountains of central Peru, where other groups were already living. The newcomers, known as the Inca, were nothing special at first, but they slowly became more powerful. Then, in 1438, a group called the Chanka attacked the Inca. The result would be a family feud and the birth of an empire.

At the time of the Chanka attack, the Inca leader was Wiraqocha Inka. He was said to be a brave fighter who had vowed to conquer half the world, but when the attack came he fled, taking three of his four sons with him. The fourth son, Inka Yupanki, stayed and fought the Chanka. He won the battle, captured the Chanka leaders, and invited his father to wipe his feet on the prisoners, a sign of victory.

Wiraqocha refused. The foot-wiping honor, he said, should go to Yupanki's older brother, Inka Urqon—who was also Wiraqocha's heir. This angered Yupanki. He said he had not captured the Chanka warriors just so his brother could step on them. The fight between Wiraqocha and Yupanki got out of hand, and Wiraqocha decided to murder his difficult younger son. Wiraqocha's plan failed, however, and he left the Inca territory in shame.

Yupanki remained in charge of the Inca. He took a new name, Pachakuti, which meant "Worldshaker" in the Inca language. Then he went about conquering everything in sight. For 25 years, Pachakuti steadily enlarged the Inca empire. Then the Worldshaker handed the job of conquest over to his son Thupa Inka, while he turned his own attention to rebuilding Qosqo. Pachakuti wanted the former village to become the capital of a glorious empire.

THE GOLDEN CENTER OF THE UNIVERSE

At the heart of the new Qosqo was a huge open plaza called Awkaypata. It was carpeted with white sand carried from the Pacific coast. Every day, an army of city workers raked the sand. Around the plaza rose temples and the homes of nobles. These buildings were made of immense stone blocks and covered with sheets of polished gold. When the sun struck the golden walls and white sand floor of Awkaypata, the plaza brimmed with light.

To the Inca, Awkaypata was more than the center of their growing empire. It was the center of the whole universe. Four highways led out from the plaza. They marked the sections of the Inca empire, which Pachakuti called Tawantinsuyu, "Land of the Four Quarters."

Pachakuti also designed the empire's social and economic system. For centuries, villagers in the highlands had spent part of their time working in teams on community

Pachakuti turned community service into the backbone of the empire's economy.

SACRED SPIT

The Inca believed their emperors were sacred, set apart from the rest of the world. Everything the emperor touched was collected and stored so that ordinary people could not touch it. Even the emperor's saliva could not touch the ground. If he had to spit, he did it into a courtier's hand. The courtier wiped the saliva with a special cloth, and stored it. Once a year, everything the emperor had touched was burned in a ceremony.

HUASCAR-INCA, INCA XIII.

Above: Washkar, also known as Huascar

projects, such as repairing irrigation ditches. Pachakuti turned community service into the backbone of the empire's economy. He declared that all land and property belonged to the emperor. Everyone regularly had to spend time working for the state, whether mining, farming, herding, building roads, or making pots in state factories. Sometimes crews were away from home for months on end, fulfilling their service. During this time the state fed, clothed, and housed them with goods supplied by other work crews.

The state moved people in and out of every job that needed doing. It also moved whole populations around the empire. When Tawantinsuyu took over a new area, the Inca moved many people from other parts of the empire into the new territory. The newcomers and the original inhabitants were forced to communicate using Runa Simi, not their native languages. The goal was to replace local cultures and customs with a single empire-wide culture—the culture of Tawantinsuyu.

FIGHTING FOR THE FRINGE

Pachakuti died peacefully in 1471. His son Thupa Inka took the "crown," a length of colored, braided cloth with a red tasseled fringe over the forehead that the Inca ruler wore as a headband.

By this time, the emperor was considered sacred. The blood of the royal Inca was believed to be so special that the only mate worthy of producing an heir was another royal Inca. That's why Thupa Inka began the practice of rulers marrying their sisters. (He had many other wives, as well.)

By the time Thupa Inka died in 1493, he ruled the biggest empire on earth. In addition, from all his wives, he also had more than 60 sons. His death set off a fight for the royal fringe between two of them. The winner was still a teenager when he became emperor under the name Wayna Qhapaq. Later, he killed two of his own brothers, to avoid future family conflicts. Then he married one of his sisters.

Around 1520, Wayna Qhapaq led an army north to conquer Ecuador for the empire. The people of the wet tropical forests did not share the Andean culture and were not interested in joining it. They resisted ferociously, but after a long struggle, the Inca won. Wayna Qhapaq stayed in Ecuador, enjoying the warm climate and the soft clothing made of vampire-bat wool. When he died in 1526, two of his sons, Washkar and Atawallpa, wanted the royal fringe. Washkar married one of his sisters to strengthen his claim to be the new emperor, but civil war was unavoidable.

The brutal war between Washkar and Atawallpa lasted three years and crisscrossed the Andes. At one point, Washkar's forces captured Atawallpa, but one of Atawallpa's wives helped him escape. Atawallpa then shattered Washkar's army and made a drinking cup from the skull of Washkar's main general.

In the summer of 1532, Atawallpa's generals captured Washkar in an ambush. While they executed Washkar's wives and children, Atawallpa slowly marched toward Qosqo at the head of a huge, triumphant procession.

PALE, HAIRY PEOPLE ON ANIMALS

In the fall, Atawallpa's victory procession stopped outside the small city of Cajamarca. There, Atawallpa learned a strange piece of news. Pale, hairy people who sat on enormous animals had landed on the coast.

Atawallpa decided to wait for these strangers to arrive in Cajamarca. The strangers were 168 Spanish men, led by a conquistador named Francisco Pizarro. After they reached Cajamarca, they persuaded Atawallpa to visit them in the central square of the town. Atawallpa approached the square with 5,000 to 6,000 of his soldiers.

The Incan soldiers, approaching in friendship, carried only ceremonial weapons. Still, there were so many of them that the waiting Spanish wet themselves with terror, according to Pedro Pizarro, the conquistador's younger brother, who was there. Francisco Pizarro, however, had cleverly hidden Spanish guns and horses just inside the buildings surrounding the square. A Spanish priest handed Atawallpa a travel-stained prayer book. Atawallpa threw the book aside. It meant nothing to him. The Inca had insulted a Christian book, though, which gave the Spanish the excuse they needed to attack.

Guns roared, and horses charged out of the buildings. The smoke and fire and giant, plunging animals—like nothing the Inca had ever seen—threw Atawallpa's army into

> The Inca had insulted a Christian book, which gave the Spanish the excuse they needed to attack.

Left: The conquistador Francisco Pizarro
seizing the Inca king Atawallpa

confusion and panic. Hundreds were trampled to death as they tried to flee the square. The Spanish seized the advantage and killed most of the others. Pizarro himself, it was said, captured Atawallpa.

THE BROKEN PROMISE

Atawallpa was a prisoner, but he still commanded the Inca empire. Seeing that the Spanish were obsessed with precious metals, Atawallpa promised to fill a large room with gold and two rooms with silver in exchange for his freedom. Pizarro agreed.

Atawallpa ordered his generals to strip Qosqo of its silver and gold. He also told them to kill Washkar, so that the way would be clear for Atawallpa to become emperor as soon as the ransom was paid and he was free.

For months, the road from Qosqo to Cajamarca was crowded with caravans of llamas carrying precious jewelry, sculpture, and ornaments ripped from buildings. The rooms slowly filled with gold and silver. By May 1533, they were full. Atawallpa had kept his part of the bargain. Pizarro melted all the artworks down into gold and silver bars to be shipped to Spain. Then, instead of releasing Atawallpa as he had promised, Pizarro had him strangled.

The conquistadors marched to Qosqo and seized the Inca capital. Their victory was not complete—the Inca would continue to fight the Spanish in the outlying regions of the empire for another 40 years. In a single stroke, though, a tiny force of European soldiers had overcome an army that outnumbered them by 50 times. They had brought a mighty American empire to its knees. Later, the Spanish conquerors even wrote the history of the Incan empire, based on interviews with surviving Inca nobles.

Why did the Inca lose? For a long time, historians said that it was because the Spanish had two military advantages. They had steel and horses, both unknown in the Americas. Steel gave the Spanish armor, swords, guns, and cannons. Horses let the Spanish move much more quickly than the Inca, who traveled on foot. (Llamas, the biggest beasts native to the Andes, are too small to ride.) Indeed, the sheer speed and mass of Spanish cavalry shocked the Inca—they had never seen anything like it.

Below: Atawallpa, also known as Atahuallpa

ATAHUALLPA. INCA XIIII.

39

Pizarro melted all of the artworks down into gold and silver bars to be shipped to Spain.

Above: The conquistadors had great difficulty understanding Inca society—so much so that when they drew pictures of the Inca capital of Qosqo, they made it look like a European city, with streets in a grid. In fact, it may have been built in the outline of a puma, with the great fortress-temple of Saqsaywaman at its head.

Recent studies of Incan culture, however, have made some historians think that the Inca were not fated to be defeated in battle by the Spanish. The Inca had extremely efficient and powerful weapons: cloth slings that hurled large stones, sometimes on fire. Once the horses lost their shock value, soldiers on foot could have fought well against them—that has happened many times in history. Spanish records of the fighting in Peru reveal that the Inca overcame their surprise and killed a lot of Spanish soldiers and horses in battles and ambushes.

So maybe the Spanish didn't win just because they had steel and horses. If that is true, though, then what defeated the Inca? Perhaps the Europeans who came to Peru had some other advantage on their side, something that tipped the scales of conquest in their favor, even if they did not know it.

TOO MANY MUMMIES?

Incan society had a serious mummy problem. Like other Andean cultures, the Inca mummified their dead rulers. In addition, because they believed emperors were immortal, they treated the rulers' mummies as though they were still alive. One of Pizarro's companions witnessed a ceremony in Qosqo in which dead emperors were brought out "seated on thrones, and surrounded by pages and women with flywhisks in their hands."

Because the royal mummies were not considered dead, each mummy held on to his possessions, including his palaces and the income from the lands he had conquered. Each dead ruler's courtiers or descendants were represented by female spirit mediums who claimed to speak for the immortal emperors. Each one of the mummified emperors—or his living representatives—fought for power and rank in the political life of the empire. Qosqo was so crowded with palaces that when Wayna Qhapaq came to power, there was no room for him to build a home on Awkaypata, Qosqo's sacred square. His undead ancestors had used up all the real estate.

PART TWO
WHY DID EUROPE SUCCEED?

THE SAME STORY APPEARS OVER AND OVER AGAIN IN history books about the European conquest of the Americas. Time after time, a small group of Europeans defeated a much larger population of Native Americans. Why did the Europeans always win?

Indians had no horses, guns, or armor— indeed, they were often terrified by their first sight of men on horses or exploding cannons. Were those things the key to victory? Or did Europeans succeed in taking over the Americas because of forces outside their control and outside the control of the Native American nations they conquered?

CHAPTER 5

THE GREAT MEETING

NOVEMBER 8, 1519, WAS A TURNING POINT IN THE HISTORY OF THE world. On that day, several hundred Spanish adventurers rode their horses into a city unlike any place they had ever seen or heard of. It was so much bigger and richer than any city in Europe that the Spanish gaped in awe at the dazzling scene.

Less than two years later, the Spanish had conquered that city, even though their numbers were few and the city was the capital of a mighty American empire. A small, vastly outnumbered force had taken over a huge, highly advanced, and rich empire with a ferociously tough army.

The Europeans won in Mexico. Their weapons and battle tactics were not superior to those of the Native Americans, but they were different. The same thing would happen 13 years later in Peru, when Pizarro conquered the Inca. Why did it happen again and again?

A CITY OF MYSTERY

The city that the Spanish entered in 1519 was Tenochtitlán. It sat in the heart of Mexico, a warm, fertile basin fringed with mountains. In the middle of the basin sparkled the clear, clean water of Lake Texcoco, 50 miles long. Tenochtitlán was not the first great capital to enjoy this magnificent setting. A thousand years earlier, a massive stone city had risen near the lake's northeastern shore.

Opposite: A detail from artist Diego Rivera's mural of market day in Tenochtitlán with the Great Temple in the background

Above: The great city of Teotihuacán was organized around a wide, ten-mile-long avenue now called the Avenue of the Dead. Toward one end were two enormous pyramids (*Pyramid of the Sun, left*).

No one knows what the people who built that first city called it. Hundreds of years later, people gave it the name Teotihuacán, and that is how we know it today. Teotihuacán started as just a small village, one of many in the area. About 2,000 years ago, it began to gain military power. Four centuries later, Teotihuacán ruled most of central Mexico. The village had grown into a capital city of more than 200,000 people—an enormous urban center for that time.

The city was organized around the Avenue of the Dead, a wide street that cut across the landscape as straight as an ax stroke. The Pyramids of the Sun and Moon towered over the avenue's north end. The Pyramid of the Sun was the world's third largest pyramid, and it sat on top of a deep cave. To the people of the city, the cave may have been a sacred site, the place where humans first came out of the earth. About a mile away, along the avenue, was the huge, sprawling Temple of the Feathered Serpent, home of Teotihuacán's rulers.

The empire of Teotihuacán was famous and powerful, yet we know little about it. Even the language spoken by its people is unknown. The city's occupants left some writing, but archaeologists have not yet decoded it. They do know that Teotihuacán fell in the sixth century AD, but the cause of its downfall is a mystery. All that remains are the huge ruins of the capital, an hour's drive from modern Mexico City.

THE EAGLE ON THE CACTUS

The empire of Teotihuacán was gone, but it left a lasting mark on central Mexico. Societies that came later modeled themselves on Teotihuacán. They liked to think that they had inherited its imperial glory.

The first heirs of Teotihuacán were the Toltec. They rose to power 500 years after the fall of Teotihuacán, but their empire did not last long. The Toltec civilization collapsed around AD 1200. Its fall created an opening for new powers in central Mexico. Half a dozen groups from the northern and western desert moved into the basin. One of these groups was the Mexica.

Poor and powerless, the Mexica were an unlikely choice to inherit imperial glory. In fact, the Mexica were driven away from the best, most fertile territories on the lakeshore by more powerful enemies. Centuries later, the grandson of the last Mexica ruler told the story of what happened after the Mexica fled to a swampy, uninhabited island on the west side of the lake.

The Mexica wandered around the island for days, he wrote, looking for food and a place to settle, until one of the priests had a vision in a dream. Huitzilopochtli, the patron deity of the Mexica, appeared and told the people to search the swamp for a *tenochtli*—a cactus. On that cactus, the god promised, they would see an eagle warming itself in the sun. The next morning, the people did find a cactus with an eagle sitting on it. At that spot, they founded their city, which they called Tenochtitlán.

At first, the new city-state did not amount to much. A stronger city-state on the shore dominated the Mexica, who had to send men to fight that other state's wars. About a century after the founding of Tenochtitlán, though, things changed for the better, thanks to two Mexican rulers, Itzcoatl and his nephew Tlacaelel. Itzcoatl was the *tlatoani*, the ruler in charge of wars and relations with other states. Tlacaelel was the *cihuacoatl*, in charge of the internal government of the state, but he was really the more powerful of the two, ruling Tenochtitlán from behind the scenes for more than 50 years.

Teotihuacán was a city of more than 200,000 people—an enormous urban center for that time.

Triple Alliance, AD 1519

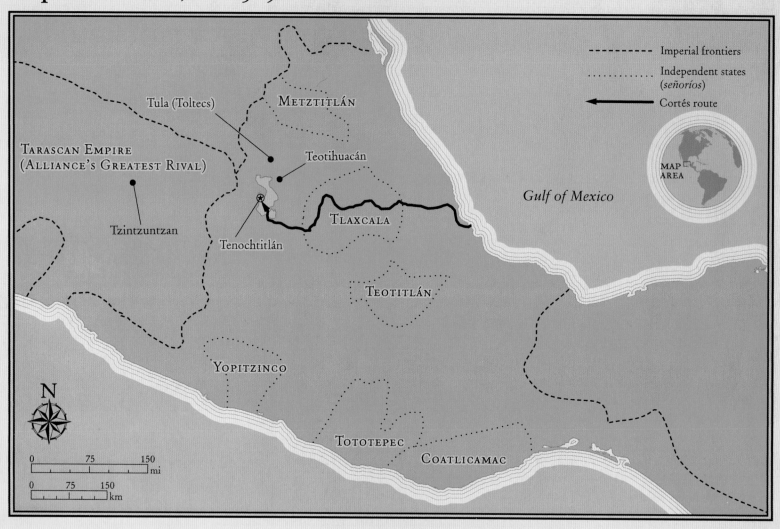

Imperial frontiers

Independent states (*señoríos*)

Cortés route

MAP AREA

Tula (Toltecs)

METZTITLÁN

Teotihuacán

Tarascan Empire (Alliance's Greatest Rival)

Gulf of Mexico

Tzintzuntzan

Tenochtitlán

Tlaxcala

Teotitlán

Yopitzinco

Tototepec

Coatlicamac

N

0   75   150
mi

0   75   150
km

In 1428, Tlacaelel had the idea of joining Tenochtitlán in an alliance with two other small, underdog city–states to overthrow their overlords. The plan worked. The three victorious states called themselves the Triple Alliance—with the Mexica the most powerful of the three. (The Triple Alliance is most often called the Aztec empire, but the term *Aztec* was popularized by European writers in the nineteenth century. It was never used by Triple Alliance members to refer to themselves.)

Tlacaelel was a visionary and patriot who believed that the Mexica would one day rule a vast empire. To do so, the Mexica needed two things: a glorious past and a sacred mission. Tlacaelel set about to create both.

The real past of the Mexica was one of poverty and humiliation. To hide that awkward fact (not just from other states but also from the Mexica themselves), Tlacaelel ordered the priests to burn their people's written histories. They then wrote new ones full of great deeds. Tlacaelel also put forward an elaborate new religious mythology. It made Huitzilopochtli into the sun, whose survival was vital to the fate of all people. In this mythology, the Mexica had a sacred duty to conquer the world for Huitzilopochtli.

Another of Tlacaelel's creations may have been history's first large-scale program of mandatory education. Every male citizen had to go to school until he was 16. This emphasis on learning was part of a great flowering of poetry and philosophy. More writings survive in Nahuatl, the language of the Triple Alliance, than in the language of the famous Greek thinkers of the ancient world.

FEEDING THE SUN

The sun's job was terribly hard, the Mexica believed. Every day as the sun rose in the sky, it had to battle the moon and stars, and its life-giving light was a victory that must be won again the next day. The people could strengthen the sun for its battles with the stars, though. They could feed it chalchíhautl, the energy of life. There was only one way to do this: human sacrifice.

Slaves or criminals could be sacrificed to the sun, but most victims offered were prisoners of war. As the Mexica saw it, the Triple Alliance's wars of conquest were not simply to enlarge the empire—they were to provide food for the sun, to keep the universe alive. The ceremonies of sacrifice were public religious rituals that reminded people of this spiritual goal. The Triple Alliance may have sacrificed 3,000 or 4,000 people a year. Europeans were appalled, but it is important to note that sixteenth-century England, France, and Spain executed many more people than the Mexica did, relative to the size of their populations, and many of those executions were performed before huge crowds. From our perspective, the Europeans and the Triple Alliance were surprisingly alike—violent death was part of the social landscape on both sides of the Atlantic.

Above: Hernán Cortés receives gifts of meat and other goods from a local chieftain who became an ally of the Spanish.

"THIS BARBARIAN LORD"

In its first 90 years, the Triple Alliance grew rich and powerful. Then, on April 22, 1519, a Spanish conquistador named Hernán Cortés landed on the east coast of Mexico, near where the city of Veracruz now stands. He and his men had come from Spain's colonies in the Caribbean Sea, looking for new lands to conquer.

Cortés was not just a swashbuckling soldier. He was also a shrewd politician. He knew that he would have to understand how the empire of Mexico was organized if he wanted to bring it down.

As Cortés studied the Triple Alliance, he saw that it was anything but unified. It was a patchwork of states that were dominated to different degrees by the Triple Alliance. Some states had managed to remain independent of the Alliance, even though they were surrounded by Alliance territory. Other states had bowed to the superior strength of the Alliance, but they were bitter and resentful. Cortés saw that the empire of the Triple Alliance was seething with discontent. He would later use this discontent for his own purposes.

As the Spanish moved inland, they fought battle after battle with Tlaxcala, a group of four small kingdoms that had managed to remain independent from the Triple Alliance. The Tlaxcala warriors greatly outnumbered the Spanish, but the Spanish had horses, guns, and steel swords. These advantages helped the Spanish win each battle, but they lost men with every fight.

Just as Cortés faced a final defeat, the Tlaxcala kings offered him a deal. They would stop attacking the Spanish if Cortés would join them in an attack on the hated Triple

Alliance. Cortés agreed, and the Spanish rode on toward Tenochtitlán at the head of an army of up to 20,000 Tlaxcalans. When the Spanish reached the capital of the Triple Alliance, the tlatoani, Motecuhzoma, didn't want them to enter the city. He took no action to keep them out, however, and they ignored his protests.

Tenochtitlán was a marvel to the Spanish. Built on a cluster of islands (mostly man-made) in Lake Texcoco, the city was crisscrossed by canals and linked to the mainland by three long causeways. Hundreds of boats flitted like butterflies through the canals and across the water of the lake, carrying people and goods to the city's crowded markets. Immense colored banners draped the buildings. Gardens were everywhere—there was nothing like them in the cities of Europe. Even more remarkable were the wide boulevards. The streets of European cities ran ankle-deep with sewage, but in Tenochtitlán a thousand men worked just to keep the streets spotless.

All the wealth and power of the empire flowed into the hands of Motecuhzoma, as Cortés later explained to the king of Spain. The conquistador wrote, "Can there be anything more magnificent than that this barbarian lord should have all the things to be found under the heavens in his domain, fashioned in gold and silver and jewels and feathers?"

Impressed as he was, Cortés also realized that with a single word, Motecuhzoma could order his army to wipe out even the memory of the Spanish. So they seized the tlatoani in his own palace. This act horrified the Mexica, who regarded their ruler as a representative of the gods. Uncertain how to respond to the captivity of their ruler in his own palace, the Mexica waited seven months before they mounted an attack on the invaders.

Fearing the worst, Motecuhzoma begged his people to leave the Spanish alone. He was killed soon afterward. Mexican accounts say that the Spanish murdered him. Spanish accounts say that his own countrymen killed him. Either way, the battle was on.

A vigorous new tlatoani named Cuitlahuac led the Mexica against Cortés and his men. The Mexica

Below: Collapsed carving of a skull rack, which was used to store the heads of slain enemy warriors. The rack in Tenochtitlán horrified the Spanish invaders because it held more than 10,000 heads.

Above: In a fierce battle that raged throughout the city, the people of Tenochtitlán drove out the Spanish invaders.

forced the Spanish into narrow alleyways, where their horses and guns were little help to them. Under a hail of spears, darts, and arrows, the Spanish retreated in panic across the causeways. In a single night's fighting, the Mexica had defeated Cortés totally, killing three-quarters of his men. They did not kill Cortés, though, which was a costly mistake.

CORTÉS THE CONQUEROR

Cortés never even considered giving up. Turning to some of the other states under the control of the Triple Alliance, he got them to join him and Tlaxcala. These new alliances gave him a fighting force of about 200,000. Cortés also cooked up a clever plan for attacking Tenochtitlán.

Knowing that the Mexica could easily defend the narrow causeways leading into the city, Cortés decided to approach from a different direction. He ordered 13 large ships to be built on the shore of the lake. This time, he would strike at Tenochtitlán from the water.

When Cortés and his Indian allies attacked, the Mexica resisted fiercely. As many as 100,000 people died in the fighting. In the end, Cortés managed to take the city, but only by destroying most of it. On August 21, 1521, the Triple Alliance surrendered. The last heir to Teotihuacán had fallen.

The bold and determined Cortés went down in history as the conqueror of Mexico. It wasn't superior technology that gave him the victory, though. Horses, guns, and swords hadn't prevented the Mexica from driving Cortés out of their city once. His second attack succeeded only because he had a huge army of Indian allies, whose leaders wanted to use the Spanish to help them destroy the Triple Alliance. Even this enormous force might not have been enough to overcome Tenochtitlán if something else hadn't happened while he was supervising the building of his ships on the shore of Lake Texcoco.

In his victory over the Triple Alliance, Cortés had allies. The Tlaxcala and other Indians fought on his side. The same thing happened when Pizarro fought the Inca. He got help against Atawallpa from Washkar's followers, who had lost the civil war, and from other people the Inca had conquered. A lot of Indians hated the Triple Alliance and the Inca and were glad to help someone get rid of them.

In both cases, though, something else was going on. The Spanish had more allies than they knew. The powerful but invisible forces of geography and genetics were on their side. To understand how these forces helped the Europeans defeat the Native Americans, we must look back in time to when the first people arrived in the Americas.

Above: Located on a set of islands in a lake, the Triple Alliance capital of Tenochtitlán was an aquatic city, fed by a network of floating gardens (*right*) and thronged by small boats carrying goods and people through the many canals between islands.

CHAPTER 6

LONG, LONG AGO

WE KNOW NATIVE AMERICANS FIRST CAME TO THE AMERICAS from somewhere in the "Old World" of Africa, Europe, and Asia. What we don't know is when. Experts have argued about it for many decades. Each discovery seems to push the arrival of people in the Americas further back in time.

WHO WERE THE FIRST AMERICANS?

At the end of the fifteenth century, Christopher Columbus showed Europeans the way to the Americas. Columbus didn't realize what he found. He went to his grave claiming that he had landed on the shores of Asia, near India. That's why he called the people he found there "Indians." He was wrong, but the name stuck.

As soon as Europeans realized that the Americas were not part of Asia, they attempted to determine where the Indians had come from. The Native Americans didn't fit the view of world history that most Europeans shared in the sixteenth century (and for some time afterward). This view of history came from the Christian Bible, which said that all human beings and animals drowned in Noah's flood, except for those on the ark. The passengers on the ark were believed to be the ancestors of all living things on Earth. The ark was thought to have landed in the mountains of Turkey. It was easy to see how people and animals had spread from there to Africa, Asia, and Europe. But how had

Opposite: Columbus's landing in the Americas, as dramatized by the early twentieth-century illustrator, William J. Aylward

Above: Although pictographs are found in hundreds of sites in Texas and the southwest, their exact meaning is often unclear. Laboratories have carbon-dated a few pictographs, some of which are apparently as old as 12,000 years.

those people and animals manage to cross the oceans and populate the Americas?

One of the first to tackle the question was a Roman Catholic teacher named José de Acosta, who spent 25 years in Spain's Mexico colony. In 1590, Acosta wrote that the Indians, like all humans, had to be descendants of the biblical first man, Adam. This meant that the Indians must have originated in the Old World and then walked to the Americas. If people had walked to the Americas, Acosta wrote, America and Asia "must join somewhere." Hundreds of years later, scientists would prove him right.

In the meantime, though, Europeans kept trying to figure out which group of Europeans or Asians had been the ancestors of the Indians. People had all sorts of ideas. The Indians could have descended from ancient Egyptians, Greeks, Romans, or Jewish tribes. A few people even claimed that the Native Americans were the last survivors of the mythical lost continent of Atlantis.

Then, in the nineteenth century, the remains of ancient human ancestors began to turn up in Europe. Scientists started to understand that people had been living in Europe since the ice ages, when glaciers covered the northern lands, tens or even hundreds of thousands of years ago. Consequently, if early humans had lived in Europe during the ice ages, maybe humans also inhabited the Americas at the same time. People started searching the Americas for evidence of these ancient inhabitants.

Right: Clovis (*right*) and Folsom (*far right*) spear points were found in early Indian sites throughout the United States, Mexico, and Canada.

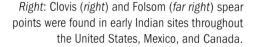

ANCIENT AMERICANS

By the 1890s, amateur archaeologists had found stone tools and old bones in many parts of the United States. The discoverers believed that they had found traces of Ice Age Americans, but the country's top archaeologists and geologists disagreed. There was no proof, they said, that the stones and bones were more than a few hundred years old, or a few thousand at most. Then a flash flood in New Mexico changed everything.

The flood tore a new gully into the ground near the town of Folsom, exposing huge bones. In 1926, a Colorado museum director named Jesse Figgins began to excavate those bones. He hoped to find a big bison skeleton for his museum, but he found much more.

Figgins's workers uncovered human artifacts—several well-made stone spear points. A piece from one of the spear points was pressed into the dirt around a bison bone. To Figgins, this meant that a human hunter had lived at the same time as the bison. That kind of bison became extinct more than 10,000 years ago, though. If the find was genuine, it would mean that the history of human beings in the Americas stretched far into the past.

The next year, a panel of top archaeological observers traveled to Folsom. They watched Figgins unearth a spear point from between two ribs of an ancient bison. The evidence was clear. People had lived in the Americas during a time that geologists call the Pleistocene epoch, which ended 10,000 years ago.

Two hundred miles south of Folsom, in another New Mexico village called Clovis, lived a teenager named Ridgely Whiteman. Whiteman, who was part Indian, was fascinated by Indian lore and the archaeological excitement in Folsom. In 1929, when Whiteman was 19, he discovered large bones sticking out of the ground near Clovis. His find led to another major discovery. During the 1930s, excavators at Clovis found artifacts from *two* early cultures.

They found a layer of stone tools just like those at Folsom. But buried beneath these Folsom-like artifacts was another layer of tools that were bigger, thicker, and slightly cruder. The two layers were a good example of one of archaeology's basic principles, stratigraphy. It deals with the strata, or layers, of the Earth. New layers get deposited

GEORGE McJUNKIN AND THE BIG BONES

Born a slave before the Civil War, George McJunkin had no formal education. He didn't learn to read until he was an adult. McJunkin had taught himself to play the violin, however, and he knew a lot about astronomy, geology, and biology. McJunkin worked as a ranch foreman near Folsom, New Mexico. After a flash flood, he was the first to notice big animal bones sticking out of the ground. McJunkin knew the bones did not belong to any living species. He tried for years to get local people interested in his discovery. Thanks to his efforts, the bones eventually came to the attention of Figgins and other scientists—but McJunkin did not live to see his discovery become famous. He died in 1922, a few years before the Folsom finds made headlines.

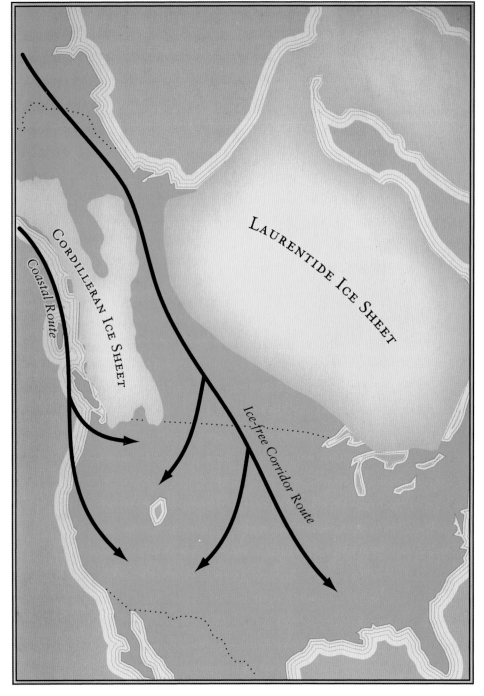

Above: In 1964, archaeologist C. Vance Haynes proposed that the first Americans migrated across the exposed floor of the Bering Strait and through an ice-free corridor created by the melting of the two great ice sheets that covered the northern half of the continent.

on top of old ones. In other words, as you dig deeper, the soil layers get older, and so do any fossils or artifacts they contain.

Stratigraphy is not always straightforward. Earthquakes and flowing water can mix up the order of layers. Clovis was dry and stable, though, so its stratigraphy was not complicated. The bigger tools were found below the Folsom tools, so they were older. The people who had made these older tools became known as the Clovis culture. They came before the Folsom culture—but when exactly did they live? No one knew, because geological layers could not be dated precisely before radiocarbon dating. Archaeologists discovered many more Folsom and Clovis sites throughout North America.

PASSAGE TO AMERICA

One of the first things scientists did when radiocarbon dating was invented in the 1950s was to determine the age of the Clovis culture. Radiocarbon dating doesn't work on stone tools, but it can be used to date bone and wood. Testing confirmed that all of the Clovis sites were occupied between 13,500 and 12,900 years ago.

One of the archaeologists who worked on the radiocarbon dating was C. Vance Haynes. The Clovis dates had special meaning to Haynes, because he had training in geology. He realized that the Clovis culture appeared in the Americas just after the only time period in which people could have walked to Alaska from Siberia, the northeastern corner of Asia.

Today, an arm of the Pacific Ocean called the Bering Strait separates Siberia and Alaska. It is only 56 miles wide and 120 feet deep, shallower than many lakes. During the ice ages, however, so much of the world's water was frozen into glaciers that the level of the oceans fell as much as 400 feet. During that time, a broad, flat bridge of dry land that geologists call Beringia linked Siberia and Alaska.

Animals, and the people who hunted them, could have walked from Siberia across Beringia to Alaska. When they got to western Canada, though, they would have run into two massive ice sheets that made travel impossible. This icy barrier prevented the colonization of the Americas—except for one short period of time.

The ice ages drew to a close about 15,000 years ago. The climate warmed, the glaciers slowly melted, and the sea rose. It took about 3,000 years for Beringia to be completely covered with water. During these 3,000 years, as the edges of the two great Canadian ice sheets melted, a pathway opened between them. Geologists call this pathway the ice-free corridor. It led south along the Yukon River and the eastern side of the Rocky Mountains. While the Pacific Ocean was slowly swallowing Beringia, animals and people could have migrated across the land bridge and down the ice-free corridor into the center of North America. Once Beringia was under the waves, though, the migration ended.

In 1964, Haynes published his theory about the peopling of the Americas. He claimed that the first humans had arrived in North America between 14,000 and 13,000 years ago, by way of Beringia and the ice-free corridor. They spread out through North America and became the original Paleoindians, or ancient Indians—the Clovis culture. All the Indians of the Americas were descended from the Clovis people.

Haynes's theory quickly gained hold in both the scientific community and the public imagination. For years, it

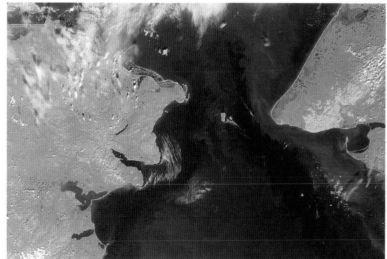

Above: Satellite image of the Bering Strait

THE MYSTERIOUS SKELETONS OF LAGOA SANTA

Thirty human skeletons were jumbled up with the bones of huge, extinct beasts! It could have been one of the scientific finds of the century—the nineteenth century, that is. A Danish plant collector found the bones in the early 1840s in caves near a village called Lagoa Santa, in Brazil. He sent most of the skeletons to a museum in Denmark, thinking they would soon be studied. Instead, they remained in boxes for more than 100 years.

When scientists finally examined the Lagoa Santa skeletons in the 1960s, some argued that the skeletons were different from most Native American remains. For one thing, the Lagoa Santa skulls have heavy brows above the eye sockets. Tests suggested that the skeletons could be as much as 15,000 years old. They might be the oldest human remains in the Americas.

Some researchers think that the Lagoa Santa people might have been the ancestors of the Botocudo, Brazilian natives who were wiped out when Portugal colonized Brazil. With their bulging brows, the Botocudo looked different from other Indians. These researchers are now searching for genetic information about the Botocudo. Were they unrelated to modern Indians? If so, where did they come from? The Lagoa Santa skeletons also look something like Aborigines, the native people of Australia. Could this mean that Aborigines made their way to the Americas thousands of years ago? Only further study will solve the mysteries of Lagoa Santa's skeletons.

was the standard vision of how people came to the Americas. Anyone who claimed to have found human relics older than the Clovis culture was ignored or called a crackpot, often for good reason. Then, in the 1980s, new ideas started to threaten the Clovis-first theory.

WORDS, TEETH, AND DNA

The first crack in the theory came from a study of Native American languages. Joseph H. Greenberg was a linguist, a scholar who studies language. He spent 40 years comparing hundreds of Indian languages and found that they belonged to three large language families: Aleut in the far north, Na-Dené in western Canada and the American Southwest, and Amerind everywhere else.

In Greenberg's view, the three language families represented three separate migrations to the Americas. The ancestors of the Amerind-speakers came first, sometime before 11,000 years ago. Around 9,000 years ago, the ancestors of the Na-Dené speakers arrived. The Aleut people came last, about 4,000 years ago. This did not mean that the Clovis-first theory had to be wrong, but it was a sign that the picture of Native American origins was more complicated than people had thought.

Greenberg's three-migrations theory was backed up by evidence from Indians' teeth. All humans have the same number and type of teeth, but there are many tiny differences from one ethnic group to the next. A scientist named Christy G. Turner II examined more than 200,000 Indian teeth and found that they fell into three main groups that matched Greenberg's language families. Turner also compared Amerind teeth with Siberian teeth and claimed that the Amerinds had split off from the Siberians about 14,000 years ago.

For more insight into Native American origins, some researchers turned to the fast-growing science of genetics. By 1990, they had discovered that almost all Indians belong to one of four genetic categories called haplogroups. Three of the Indian haplogroups are also very common in Siberia. This confirms that American Indians came from Asian ancestors.

The next step was to compare the DNA of different Indian groups to see how long ago they had split off from their shared ancestors. The results were surprising. One genetic study suggested that the first migration to the Americas took place sometime between 29,545 and 22,414 years ago—at least 10,000 years before Clovis. Earlier studies had shaken the Clovis-first theory, but the genetic evidence argued strongly that the Clovis people were *not* the first Americans.

Another group of researchers focused on the one Indian haplogroup that is very rare in Siberia. They decided that there had been only one migration from Asia, and that it must have contained, by chance, some members of that rare haplogroup. The migrants left Asia between 43,000 and 33,000 years ago scientists concluded. Soon after arriving in Beringia, they split up. Some went south, into North America—*before* the two great Canadian ice sheets joined. The rest stayed in Beringia for thousands of years. Then, at the close of the ice ages, they also went south, in one or two waves. According to this

Genetic evidence suggested that the first migration to the Americas took place at least 10,000 years before Clovis.

theory, just one group of Paleoindians colonized the Americas, but they arrived in several separate migrations.

The genetic studies raised more questions. Archaeologists could not judge whether the genetic evidence was solid. Even genetics experts disagreed about the date and number of migrations and about where in Asia the migrants had come from. Only one thing was clear: The Clovis-first theory was drastically weakened and not just by the genetic studies. A controversial new archaeological find also suggested that Paleoindians lived in the Americas before Clovis.

Above: Child's footprint found in the Monte Verde deposit

A DISCOVERY IN SOUTH AMERICA

Monte Verde is a boggy riverbank in the South American nation of Chile. Beginning in 1977, a team led by archaeologists Mario Pino of Chile and Tom Dillehay of the United States excavated a site located there. They found a settlement of tentlike shelters made of animal hides held together by poles and twisted reeds. According to Dillehay and Pino, the site was at least 12,800 years old.

If the discoverers of Monte Verde were correct, people had lived in South America nearly 13,000 years ago. The meaning of Monte Verde went much further, however. The site is 10,000 miles from the Bering Strait. Archaeologists have always believed that it would take the Paleoindians thousands of years to walk from the northern end of the Americas to the southern end. If Monte Verde was at least 12,800 years old, then humans must have arrived in the Americas thousands of years before that.

Some archaeologists, including C. Vance Haynes, the author of the Clovis-first theory, have criticized the work done at Monte Verde. They think that it and other so-called pre-Clovis sites need further study. The idea that the Clovis people were the first Paleoindians is fast fading away, however. Even geology has turned against it. In the 1990s, geologists showed evidence that the ice sheets were bigger than anyone thought and that they lasted longer. The ice-free corridor may not have been an open highway into the heart of North America after all. If Paleoindians didn't travel along the ice-free corridor, though, how did they get to the Americas?

HUGGING THE SHORE

In the 1970s, Knut Fladmark was an archaeology student in Canada. He studied the Clovis-first theory and was surprised to learn that there is very little evidence of the ice-free corridor. Fladmark started to wonder if Paleoindians had traveled down the Pacific coast of North America by boat.

Early humans did use boats. The Aborigines reached Australia from Asia by boat tens of thousands of years ago, and the Indians of the Arctic and the Pacific Northwest have long been skilled boatbuilders and seafarers. Even during the ice ages, currents of warm water from the south created pockets of mild weather along the Pacific shore of North America—islands of trees and grass in the landscape of ice. Hopping from one of these pockets to the next, Paleoindians could have made their way down the coast any time in the last 40,000 years.

There isn't any archaeological evidence for a Paleoindian migration along the coast. Maybe there never will be. When the glaciers melted thousands of years ago, rising waters covered what was then the coastline. If the first Paleoindians left traces of settlements there, they were flooded long ago. Even if no hard evidence for a coastal migration ever turns up, though, the awareness that Native Americans may have been in the Americas for 20,000 years, or even 30,000 years, seems unlikely to go away.

The ice ages made northern Europe uninhabitable until about 18,000 years ago. Britain was covered with glaciers and empty of people until about 12,500 BC. By that time, most scientists now believe, people were thriving in the Americas, from Alaska to Chile. Maybe the Americas should no longer be called "the New World."

The Americas, however, differed in an important way from the "Old World" of Africa, Asia, and Europe. People in the Americas did not share their lives with domesticated animals as they did in other parts of the world. Mystery surrounds some aspects of the relationship between animals and early humans in the Americas, but one thing we know is that livestock helped shape the different fates of the Europeans and the Native Americans.

Above: The Makah Indians have been living on the coast of what is now Washington State for more than 3,800 years.

CHAPTER 7

EXTINCTION

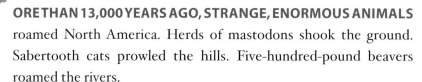

ORE THAN 13,000 YEARS AGO, STRANGE, ENORMOUS ANIMALS roamed North America. Herds of mastodons shook the ground. Sabertooth cats prowled the hills. Five-hundred-pound beavers roamed the rivers.

Unlike dinosaurs, which became extinct millions of years before humans came into existence, these huge creatures shared the Earth with people. When a massive wave of extinction passed through the Americas, though, almost all the large mammals died. The Americans had almost no animals that Paleoindians could domesticate—no cows, horses, sheep, or pigs. Most of the few surviving large mammals, such as bison and moose, refused to be domesticated. This held back the Indian cultures in some ways, but helped them in other ways.

A WORLD OF WEIRD BEASTS

Rhinoceroses and ostriches live in Africa, right? Today they do, but during the time that scientists call the Pleistocene epoch, large versions of rhinos, covered in heavy plates like armor, lived in North America. Huge, flightless birds like fierce, hungry ostriches darted swiftly across the American plains, seeking live prey.

The rhinos and ostrichlike birds were part of the Pleistocene megafauna. (The word *megafauna* means "large animals," and the Pleistocene megafauna were the large animals that lived during the Pleistocene epoch, which ended about 10,000 years ago.) They shared the landscape with beavers the size of armchairs, giant turtles that weighed almost as much as cars, and sloths that could reach tree branches 20 feet off the ground. There were also fierce dire wolves, which were larger than modern wolves.

Opposite: Woolly mammoths roamed North America, Europe, and Asia during the Pleistocene epoch.

Have you ever seen an armadillo—a small animal found in the American South that protects itself by curling up into a ball about the size of a bowling ball? During the Pleistocene, a bigger version of the armadillo lived in the Americas. It was called a glyptodont, and it was about ten feet long. If a glyptodont curled up into a ball, the ball might be taller than a person.

Sabertooth cats, dire wolves, and glyptodonts would be star attractions at zoos, if they still existed. Starting around 11,500 BC, though, the American megafauna died out. Some kinds of animals vanished completely. Others disappeared from America but continued to exist elsewhere. For example, before the Pleistocene extinctions, the Americas had three species of horse and at least two species of camel. Afterward, there were no horses in the Americas and no large camels. Only smaller members of the camel family, such as the llama and alpaca, survived in South America.

The extinction happened with amazing speed, perhaps in just a couple of centuries. What could have killed so many huge animals, so quickly? That question kicked off a scientific debate that started in the 1960s and is still going on.

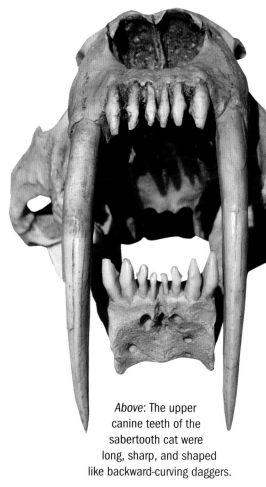

Above: The upper canine teeth of the sabertooth cat were long, sharp, and shaped like backward-curving daggers.

"A THOROUGHLY SUPERIOR PREDATOR"

As we saw in the last chapter, geologist-turned-archaeologist C. Vance Haynes published his idea in 1964 that the first humans had arrived in the Americas between 14,000 and 13,000 years ago, after crossing the Beringia land bridge from Siberia. They passed down the ice-free corridor in western Canada and became the first Paleoindians, the Clovis culture. Soon the scientific community had accepted this view of how people arrived in the Americas.

Some people noticed that the Clovis culture began just as the megafauna began to vanish, but they didn't think the two things were related. The Clovis sites that archaeologists had found had all been occupied by small bands of people. No one believed that those small bands of hunters could have created a large ecological disaster. Then, in 1967, a scientist named Paul Martin showed how the Clovis hunters could have killed off the American megafauna.

Martin was a paleontologist, a scientist who studies ancient and extinct forms of life. Extinction, he said, had to happen when beasts that had never been hunted by people were suddenly exposed to what Martin called "a new and thoroughly superior predator, a hunter who preferred killing and persisted in killing animals as long as they were available"—a human hunter, in other words.

Imagine, Martin said, that an original group of just 100 hunters crossed over Beringia and traveled down the ice-free corridor. They found themselves living in an uninhabited frontier. Historical records teach us that populations can grow very quickly on a frontier. It would have been possible for the Paleoindians to double their numbers every 20 years. This meant that their population would reach ten million in just 340 years, the blink of an eye in geological time.

A million Paleoindian hunters, Martin argued, could form a wave that would fan out from the southern end of the ice-free corridor. They would start killing animals that had never seen humans or learned to fear them. The wave of destruction would reach the Gulf of Mexico in 300 to 500 years. In 1,000 years, it would reach the southern tip of South America. To modern archaeologists, this hurricane of slaughter would show up as Clovis artifacts dating from the period when the large mammals were disappearing.

The idea that humans had hunted the Pleistocene animals into extinction was called the overkill theory. Not everyone was convinced by it. Paleontologists pointed out that many species that could not have been hunted for food also disappeared at the same time as the megafauna. Climate change, these scientists said, was

LENGTHY LIZARDS AND GIANT WOMBATS

The Americas are not the only place where Pleistocene species died out toward the end of the ice ages, between 40,000 and 10,000 years ago. Other parts of the world also lost megafauna, or large varieties of mammals, birds, and reptiles. Australia was once home to *Megalania*, a lizard that may have been up to 23 feet long, and to *Diprotodon*, a hippopotamus-sized animal that was a lot like the modern (and much smaller) marsupials known as wombats. On the nearby islands of New Zealand, the huge flightless birds called *Dinornis*, or moas, reached heights of up to 12 feet.

These and other megafauna vanished not long after the first human beings arrived and began to colonize the lands where they lived. Does this mean that the humans hunted the animals into extinction? Maybe . . . but that has not been proven, and there are other possibilities, such as climate change and disease. Scientists know that many features of life on Earth were changing as the ice ages drew to a close. The migration of humans into new territories and the disappearance of the megafauna are just two pieces of a much larger picture.

Above: This rock engraving, possibly 3,500 years old, shows a warrior with a feathered headdress. It was found in Bighorn Basin, in Wyoming.

a more likely explanation for the extinctions. Martin had an answer for them. The climate had shifted wildly during earlier periods of the Pleistocene, but that hadn't wiped out the animals. Humans, he said, had made the difference.

THE FIRST AMERICANS?

Even though not everyone agreed with the overkill theory, it created an image of the first Americans that found its way into schoolbooks, magazines, and the public mind. In this image, Paleoindians lived in small, mobile bands. Their favorite prey was the mammoth, a huge, slow-moving creature that looked like a hairy elephant. Sometimes, the Clovis hunters lured mammoths into bogs. More often, they stalked them and pelted them with spears.

Common wisdom was that Clovis people prowled their territories in search of game. They also searched for flint and other kinds of stone to use for their spear points and tools. Bands may have had as many as 50 members, with girls going outside the group to marry. Women and girls remained at camp to make clothes, tend babies, and gather plant foods, such as wild berries. Men and boys hunted, probably for days at a time.

Extinction made the big game animals grow scarce. The Clovis people had to switch from hunting mammoth to hunting bison, which were smaller but more numerous. Men gathered at watering holes to attack the bison when they came to drink, then the hunters staggered back to camp carrying loads of fresh meat.

This vision is how many archaeologists of the 1970s and 1980s pictured life in early America. Some still do. It may not have been like that at all, however. The idea that the Clovis people were the first Americans has come under attack since the 1980s, as you read in Chapter 6. Many experts now think that human beings came to the Americas thousands of years before the Clovis culture took shape—and thousands of years before the Pleistocene megafauna became extinct. If this is true, then Pleistocene people and Pleistocene megafauna lived side by side for a long time before the animals became extinct.

The overkill theory says that the Clovis culture was organized around hunting, but archaeological evidence suggests that hunting may not have been a primary activity.

Two archaeologists named David J. Meltzer and Donald K. Grayson compiled lists of everything that archaeologists found at 76 Paleoindian camps, looking for evidence of big game hunting. They found that only 14 of the camps had any evidence of big game hunting. All of that evidence came from just two species of game, the mastodon (similar to mammoths) and the bison—there were no bones of giant sloths or turtles. Maybe the Clovis people, and other early Americans as well, depended more on berries, roots, fish, and small game than on the megafauna.

LIFE WITHOUT LIVESTOCK

The Pleistocene megafauna may have died out from climate change or hunting or a deadly combination of both. Or perhaps the cause is something scientists have not yet discovered. Whatever the reason, the Pleistocene extinction had a great effect on the Indian societies that arose in the Americas.

In other parts of the world, people had a great variety of domesticated animals: cats and dogs, poultry such as chickens and ducks, and livestock such as cattle, pigs, sheep, and goats. They also had horses, the fastest form of transportation on Earth before the invention of the steam engine. The Native Americans had only a few domesticated animals, however—dogs in Mesoamerica, and in the Andes Mountains of South America the llama, the alpaca, the guinea pig, and one species of duck.

Above: Animals sinking into the mire of the La Brea tar pits. Many Ice Age animals were preserved at this California site.

Unlike the Europeans, the Indians did not live in constant contact with many animals.

The lack of livestock was one of the major differences between the Indians and the Europeans who came to the Americas. Unlike the Europeans, the Indians did not live in constant contact with many animals. This had disadvantages—without horses, for example, Indians could not travel as fast or communicate as efficiently as Europeans.

Life without livestock also had advantages. It let the Indians escape many diseases. Scientists use the term *zoonotic disease* to mean an illness that can travel from animals to humans, and there are a lot of them. Influenza is one well-known zoonotic disease. It can start in birds and migrate to people, becoming an epidemic of "bird flu." A cattle disease becomes measles in humans. When a condition called horsepox jumps to humans, it is known as smallpox. The Americas were free from these and many more zoonotic diseases. That was a blessing for the Indians who lived in isolation from the rest of the world. When the Europeans arrived, though, it became a deadly curse.

CHAPTER 8

DISEASE-FREE PARADISE?

69

REMEMBER HERNÁN CORTÉS, THE CONQUEROR OF MEXICO? When he tried to seize the capital city of Tenochtitlán, the Triple Alliance drove him out, slaughtering most of his men and horses. Cortés did not give up. He planned a second attack on the city, this time using ships. While Cortés was overseeing the building of his fleet of ships, though, the deadly disease smallpox swept through Tenochtitlán. At least a third of the city's people died, including many of its military leaders. One of them was Cuitlahuac, the tlatoani (military leader) who had led the Mexica against Cortés.

When Cortés attacked Tenochtitlán for the second time, he was at the head of a huge army of Native Americans. After fierce fighting and much bloodshed, they captured the city, but who knows how the battle would have gone if Cuitlahuac had lived? Even after all their losses, even suffering the terror and pain of a new disease, the people of Tenochtitlán fought desperately to defend their home. If their entire army had been alive and well, it might have defeated Cortés a second time. In fact, Cortes might not have found so many allies among the Indians if they thought Tenochtitlán was still strong.

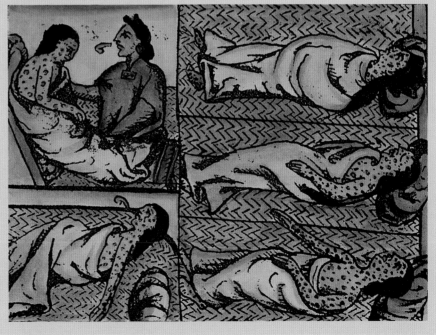

Below: In this sixteenth-century engraving, Mexica Indians infected with smallpox are spoken to by a healer.

A wave of disease passed through the Americas, wiping out whole populations of Native Americans. The same thing happened wherever Europeans landed.

The Spanish conquerors of Mexico benefited from a great and terrible wave of disease that passed through the Americas in the early sixteenth century, wiping out whole populations of Native Americans. The same thing happened again and again, wherever the Europeans landed.

HIGH RISK

The Native Americans were descended from a small group of original settlers—small compared with the large populations of Asia, Europe, and Africa. In addition, Asians, Europeans, and Africans had contact with one another over thousands of years, but the people of the Americas were cut off from the rest of the world after the sea covered the land bridge across the Bering Strait. This meant that they did not catch any of the diseases that arose in other parts of the world. Devastating illnesses such as the bubonic plague (the Black Death of the European Middle Ages) were unknown in the Americas.

In Asia, Europe, and Africa, people lived in close contact with their livestock. Native Americans, though, had almost no domesticated animals, as we saw in Chapter 7. Without livestock, Native Americans were free of the zoonotic diseases, including smallpox and measles, which spread from domesticated animals to people. In fact, the Indians had experienced almost no contagious diseases, the kind that can pass from one person to another and burn through a whole region.

Disease-free life might have seemed like paradise to Europeans, who came from a continent where outbreaks of plague killed thousands, and where every child was at risk of dying from measles or smallpox. By living with disease for so long, though, Europeans had gained some immunity, or resistance, to it. Europeans were exposed to common disease germs, usually in childhood, when they had a better chance of surviving because the childhood form of many diseases was less severe than the adult form. Some children died, but many lived. The survivors were immune to those diseases afterward, because their systems were ready to fight off the next germs they were exposed to.

Because the Indians had not grown up with European diseases, they had not acquired any immunity. This put them at high risk when they encountered disease germs. Some researchers think that the Indians were at risk for another reason, too—a reason connected with genetics.

GENETICS AND IMMUNITY

In addition to the immunity that comes from being exposed to disease, another kind of immunity is built into the body. Doctors call it the immune system, the body's way of protecting itself. Part of this job is done by tiny molecules called human leukocyte antigens (HLAs) inside most cells. The HLAs carry disease-causing materials such as viruses from the inside of the cell to the outside, where white blood cells, the body's germ police, can destroy them.

There are many types of HLAs, and each type is suited to carry certain kinds of foreign objects, such as viruses and bacteria. Your particular lineup of HLAs is called your HLA profile. It is part of your genetic heritage, passed down to you by your parents, who inherited their HLA profiles from their parents, and so on.

The more types of HLAs in a group of people, the better the chances that that group of people will be able to fight off a broad range of threats. Most human groups are a mix of many different HLA profiles. When a disease comes along, some people get sick because their HLA system can't pick out that particular kind of virus or bacteria. Other people's HLAs will present the virus or bacteria to white blood cells, so they won't get sick. If the HLA profiles

Above: This 1590 engraving shows Indians in America tending to their sick by opening the skull (*left*) to remove diseased blood and using herbal smoke (*right*) thought to offer protection from European diseases, including syphilis and smallpox.

of most people in a group are alike, then anything that makes one person sick will make most of the others sick too.

Because all Native Americans are descended from a fairly small group of distant ancestors, their genetic heritage is less mixed than in other groups. In particular, they have less variety in their HLA profiles than people from other parts of the world. A lot of Indians, in other words, have very similar sets of HLAs.

Imagine that a new disease attacks an Indian population. If the Indians' HLAs work against that disease germ, most of them will survive. If their HLAs happen to be helpless against this particular disease, though, most of them will get sick and possibly will die. This doesn't mean that Native American genes are not as good as other genes. They've simply been shaped by history, like everyone else's.

An accident of history gave Native Americans a low variety of HLA profiles. Another accident of history prevented them from being exposed to zoonotic diseases. As a result, the Indians were at high risk when the Europeans appeared. As the fate of Tenochtitlán showed, the Indians could be attacked by a new sickness at the very time they needed their strength to fight off the invaders from across the ocean.

DEATH COMES TO THE INCA

Francisco Pizarro conquered the Incan empire of South America with fewer men than Cortés had in Mexico. Like Cortés, he had the invisible power of disease working in his favor. The illness struck the Inca even before Pizarro's men marched into the empire in 1532.

The fall of the Incan empire was recorded by Pedro Cieza de León, a Spanish traveler who spent 15 years in Peru soon after the Spanish conquest. He told how, after the Inca emperor Wayna Qhapaq took sick and died in 1526, the empire fell into civil war as two sons fought over his throne. According to Cieza de León, the sickness that had killed the Incan leader was smallpox—and the emperor was not the only one to die. The disease spread through the kingdom, killing as many as 200,000 Inca, including many members of the royal family, generals, and other leaders.

Whole villages died. The countryside was a wasteland.

Wayna Qhapaq's death, and the chaos brought by the smallpox epidemic, weakened the empire so much that a handful of conquistadors could seize it. The Incan army, shattered by civil war and left largely leaderless by disease, could not mount a coordinated resistance against Pizarro. Like Cortés, Pizarro was able to acquire thousands of native allies from the Indians who hated the Inca. Pedro Pizarro, Francisco's younger brother, knew that the Spanish had been lucky. He wrote that if Wayna Qhapaq had been alive, and if the empire had not been torn by the civil war, the Spanish wouldn't have had a chance. Smallpox, not Spanish guns, horses, or leadership, defeated the Inca.

Wayna Qhapaq died six years before Pizarro landed on the coast of Peru. So where did the smallpox come from? It probably came from the Caribbean, where smallpox had broken out in the Spanish colony on the island of Hispaniola in 1518. Carried to the mainland by Spanish adventurers from the Caribbean colonies, the disease moved swiftly into central Mexico. It killed the soldiers who were defending Tenochtitlán. In the 1960s, researchers found evidence in old Spanish records that the epidemic traveled south through Central America to Ecuador, where Wayna Quapaq was living when he got sick.

In the 30 years after Pizarro's conquest of Peru, the former Inca lands suffered four more epidemics of smallpox, as well as epidemics of influenza, measles, and other European diseases. The results were terrible. "Corpses were scattered over the fields or piled up in the houses or huts," wrote a witness in 1565. Whole villages died. The countryside was a wasteland.

"A BEEHIVE OF PEOPLE"

Bartolomé de Las Casas wrote some of the most detailed descriptions of life in early Spanish Mexico. Although Las Casas went to Mexico as a conquistador, he later regretted his cruelty to the Indians. He devoted the second half of his long life to combating the harsh treatment of the Native Americans by the Spanish.

When Las Casas died in 1566, he left a history of the Spanish in America that was not published for many years because of its anti-Spanish views. According to Las Casas, the Spanish who first came to America found a crowded, bustling place—he called it "a beehive of people." To Las Casas, the Americas seemed so thick with people "that it looked as if God has placed all of the greater part of the entire human race in these countries."

Las Casas tried to calculate how many of these Native Americans died from Spanish disease and brutality. At first he wrote, "I believe, without trying to deceive myself, that it was more than fifteen million." Later, Las Casas revised the death toll upward, to forty million people. His figures may not be correct, but they tell us that the Americas had a large and thriving population. They also tell us that the arrival of the Europeans—or, more accurately, European diseases—was swiftly followed by death and disaster on an enormous scale.

DEADLY PIGS

In 1539, a few years after the fall of the Incan empire, a Spanish adventurer named Hernando de Soto landed in Florida with 600 soldiers, 200 horses, and 300 pigs. For four years, his forces wandered through what is now the American South, from the Carolinas to Texas. The Spanish were looking for gold. They didn't find any, and they wrecked everything they touched.

During their wanderings, de Soto and his followers tortured, enslaved, and killed countless Indians. However, the worst thing they did, some researchers say, was to bring those pigs.

Pigs were completely new to the Americas, but they were as important to the Spanish conquistadors as horses. Lean, hungry pigs circled the traveling troops, who fed them garbage and then killed them for meat. Pigs carry diseases, including anthrax, tuberculosis, and trichinosis, which can attack humans. Pigs can also infect other animals, such as the deer and turkey that roamed the American forests. Only a few of de Soto's pigs would have had to wander off to infect the whole forest with disease, putting Native American hunters at risk.

When de Soto crossed the Mississippi River, he found the area "thickly set with great towns" built by the Indians. More than a century later, when French explorers passed through the same region, they found only a few villages scattered along the riverbank. What had happened? One possibility is that de Soto's pigs let loose epidemics of disease that wiped out thriving cultures.

One of these cultures was the Caddo, who lived on what is now the border between Arkansas and Texas. Before de Soto, the Caddo built large public monuments such as plazas and platforms. Afterward, the survivors dug community cemeteries.

They needed those cemeteries because they were dying in great numbers. One archaeologist has estimated that there were some 200,000 Caddo before de Soto's disastrous journey through the South. A century or so later, there were about 8,500. The Caddoan population had dropped by almost 96 percent.

Opposite: Hernando de Soto "discovers" the Mississippi River in 1541.

Above: Florida Indian village, 1591

HOW MANY DIED?

Nobody knows how many Indians died in the disease epidemics of European origin that ravaged the Americas from the sixteenth century on. Most Native Americans did not keep written records. European visitors and colonists did leave accounts of disease in many writings, from private letters to the birth and death records of towns, but these sources are patchy and incomplete, and they may not always be accurate.

The question of how many Indians died of disease is related to another question: How many Indians lived in the Americas before Europeans arrived? Modern historians have answered that question in wildly different ways, always based on some degree of guesswork.

During the 1930s and 1940s, some historians suggested that only about ten million people, maybe fewer, lived in the Americas before Columbus. The majority of people lived in Central and South America, with fewer than a million in North America. Yet accounts that Europeans wrote in colonial times gave much higher numbers—as many as 40 million people in central Mexico alone, for example.

In recent decades, historians have bumped the Native American population numbers upward. Some have even claimed that the Americas were home to many more than 100 million people, more than the population of Europe. Most experts now think that this figure is too high. But few do not believe that many more Indians lived in the Americas, especially in North America, than earlier generations of historians had thought possible.

We may never know for certain how many Native Americans existed when Columbus arrived—or how many died of disease afterward. Whatever the number, the impact of the diseases changed the world. Dozens of Native American societies vanished. Cultures, ways of life, and entire peoples disappeared from the face of the earth. The Spanish, French, and English staked out their colonies, but germs were the real conquerors of the Americas.

PART THREE

WERE THE AMERICAS REALLY A WILDERNESS?

L IVING LIGHTLY ON THE LAND"—THAT'S HOW OUR schoolbooks described Native Americans for many years. Native societies like the Maya and Inca, who built big monuments and practiced large-scale farming, were striking exceptions. Most Indians, we were told, slipped through the forests and plains the same way they slipped through history, barely making a mark. Their impact on the land was so small that when Europeans arrived, they called the land a wilderness.

On the contrary, the American landscape before Columbus wasn't like that at all, a growing number of researchers say. Native peoples changed their environments—or created whole new environments—in a number of ways. Their activities shaped the landscape. Their history can still be read in the land, if you know how to look.

CHAPTER 9

AMAZONIA

ASK SIX PEOPLE TO NAME THE GREATEST WILDERNESS IN THE world today. Chances are good that some of them will answer, "The Amazon rain forest."

Hundreds of television shows and magazine articles have given us magnificent pictures of the Amazon River of South America, the vast tropical forest around it, and the wildlife that lives there. They have also shown us that today the forest is under attack by people cutting down trees to clear the land for farming, mining, and road building. Everyone has heard that the Amazonian forest is one of the world's ecological treasures, and that saving it is one of the biggest goals of the environmental movement. Researchers, however, are discovering some things about Amazonia that you probably haven't heard.

The Amazonian forest, it seems, is not a one-million-year-old wilderness, barely touched by humans, one of nature's last stands. Amazonia *is* a rare, precious, and fragile landscape, but it may not be wild. The great tropical forest may have been created by interaction between nature and human beings. If this new view of Amazonia is correct, the forest was home to large, well-organized, long-lasting Native American societies that engineered their environment in ways we are only beginning to understand.

Opposite: Amazon River

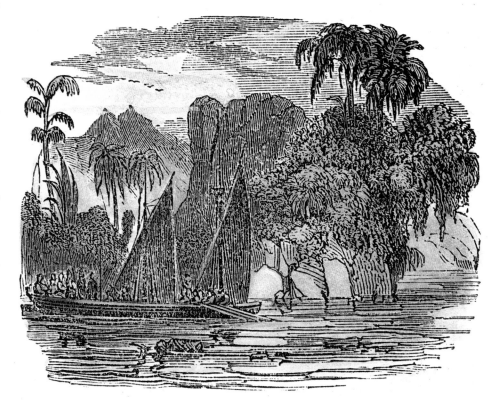

Below: A nineteenth-century drawing of Orellana's voyage down the Amazon showed the Spaniards at their ease in sailing sloops when they, in fact, were packed into a kind of big rowboat. Artists and writers often passed on overly romantic visions of the early conquistadors and some of these still shade our imaginations today.

Amazon Basin

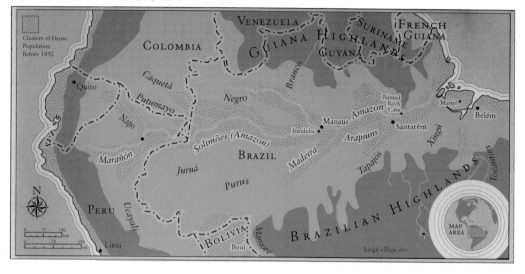

THE INCREDIBLE JOURNEY

The first written description of Amazonia comes from Gaspar de Carvajal, one of 59 Spanish adventurers who made the first journey down the Amazon River. It's difficult to know how much of Carvajal's description we should believe, because the survivors of the journey were accused of being traitors and liars.

It all started with the conquest of Peru. Francisco Pizarro, the conquistador who seized Peru, had a half brother named Gonzalo Pizarro who was a violent troublemaker. To get Gonzalo out of the way, Francisco let him set off in 1541, at the head of an expedition, to search for a legendary city of gold that was rumored to exist somewhere in the Amazon basin.

Gonzalo Pizarro led a large expedition down the eastern slope of the Andes Mountains into the wet, hot, insect-ridden forests of Amazonia. There, the Spanish blundered around for months, getting sick and starving. The forest was full of food, but they didn't know which plants were safe to eat. Finally Francisco de Orellana, Pizarro's second-in-command, volunteered to take a small group to search for supplies. They set off in a crude boat the conquistadors had built and floated down the Napo River, which flows into the Amazon.

After nine days and 600 miles on the Napo, Orellana and his men found a village with food. They stuffed themselves then decided not to make the hard journey back up the river, against the current, to carry supplies to Pizarro and the others. Instead, they would travel down the river system to the Atlantic Ocean. They knew, however, that if Pizarro was lucky enough to survive, he would call them traitors. So Carvajal decided to write the story of the trip in a way that would make it seem that they had no choice but to abandon Pizarro and the others. From the very beginning, then, Carvajal's account was untrustworthy.

Orellana and his followers took five months to float down the Amazon, the world's biggest river. Along the way, they demanded food from the native people, and usually got it. They fought with them too. Amazingly, Gonzalo Pizarro also survived the ordeal of the jungle and returned to Peru, where he accused Orellana of "the greatest cruelty that ever faithless men have shown." As for Carvajal's account of the river trip, it was not published until 1894, partly because most people didn't believe it.

Carvajal made it sound as if, at the time of his voyage, the banks of the Amazon were lined with large, populous settlements that sometimes stretched for miles. He wrote that towns dotted the riverbank, and that they were inhabited by Indians who were fierce fighters (including a tribe of women soldiers), who commanded fleets of war canoes. People in Carvajal's time thought he had made it all up. *"Mentirosa,"* one Spanish writer scoffed. "Full of lies."

Modern historians also regarded Carvajal's tales as fiction. After all, they said, Amazonia could never have supported the big, numerous communities that Carvajal described. Or could it have?

THE WET DESERT

The tropical forest of Amazonia seems so lush and dense that nothing could touch it. In fact this vibrant community of plants and animals stands on a weak foundation. Heat and intense rain have baked and pounded the nutrients out of the soil, which is so poor, eroded, and acidic that some ecologists call the tropical forest a "wet desert."

The nutrients that are missing from the soil are stored in the vegetation of the forest. When leaves or even whole trees fall, the nutritious chemicals they contain are quickly absorbed by the efficient root systems of living plants. If the land is cleared of vegetation and kept clear for a long time over a large area, the reddish soil dries out, hardens into something resembling brick, and is almost unable to support life at all.

> Carvajal made it sound as if, at the time of his voyage, the banks of the Amazon were lined with large, populous settlements that sometimes stretched for miles.

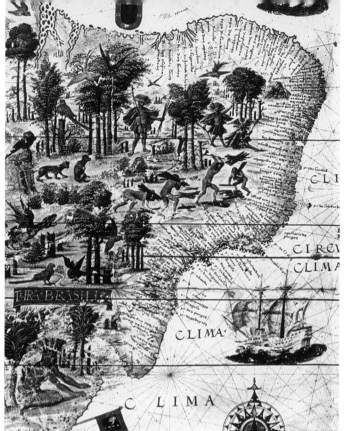

Above: Portuguese map of Brazil in 1519 showing a large number of Indian settlements

In 1971, an archaeologist named Betty Meggers published a book called *Amazonia: Man and Culture in a Counterfeit Paradise*. It explained how the people of Amazonia manage to farm in their region of poor soil and severe ecological limitations. They use a method called swidden, or slash and burn.

In swidden agriculture, farmers clear a garden plot or small field, burn the fallen trees and the cut-down brush (the ash gives the soil a quick shot of nitrogen and other nutrients), and plant their crops. They can grow food for a few years, usually three, before the jungle reclaims the plot. Then the farmer moves on to clear a new plot, giving the original one a chance to recover.

According to Meggers, this method of farming has let people scratch a living for thousands of years from a challenging environment—without destroying the ecosystem the way ordinary agriculture would. Unfortunately, swidden has other drawbacks. It sends most of the nutrients in the fallen plants up in smoke, and it adds carbon dioxide, a greenhouse gas, to the atmosphere. In addition, because swidden farmers have to pick up stakes and move to a new plot of ground every few years, they cannot live in big, permanent settlements—only villages of a few hundred people. For this reason, Meggers argued, Amazonia has only been lightly touched by the human hand.

The ideas in *Counterfeit Paradise* spread far and wide. In recent years, however, some researchers have found signs that people manipulated the Amazonian environment in the distant past, and not through swidden agriculture.

THE TREE FARMERS

One researcher in the 1970s focused on the "slash" part of slash-and-burn. Living in the world's thickest forest, the people of Amazonia had to remove a lot of trees to clear even a small plot. Many of the tree trunks were four feet thick, or more. Studies showed, however, that cutting a single four-foot tree with a stone ax—the kind of tool Native Americans had before Europeans brought steel tools to the Americas—took 115 hours.

It took 153 eight-hour days, or nearly half a year, to clear an average-sized plot.

Today, Amazonia's slash-and-burn farmers use steel axes and machetes. These can clear a plot about 20 times faster than stone tools. For this reason, some researchers now believe that maybe swidden agriculture wasn't used in Amazonia for thousands of years after all.

Swidden agriculture would have been impossible with stone tools. With all the things that farmers have to do, they simply didn't have enough time to spend months clearing fields with stone axes every few years. In fact, these researchers have argued, slash-and-burn only makes sense with steel tools. If so, then this style of farming can only be a few hundred years old. What were the Indians doing before that?

THE PRECIOUS PEACH PALM

One of the most useful trees in Amazonia is the peach palm. Tall and straight, it produces clusters of red or orange fruit full of oil, which is rich with vitamins and protein. The fruit can be boiled or smoked for eating, dried for pounding into flour, or cooked and fermented to make beer. Peach palm trees often yield two crops of fruit a year, for as long as 70 years. They are more productive per acre than maize, rice, or beans.

This wonderfully useful tree is found in many of the human-made orchards of Amazonia. It may even have been created by genetic engineering—one researcher thinks that Indians crossbred several species of palms to produce a new species with superior features. From its origins in South America, the peach palm spread north through Central America and the Caribbean. A European visitor in the seventeenth century wrote that the Native Americans valued the peach palm so much that "only their wives and children were held in higher regard."

Above: Yanomami Indian carrying peach palm fruit in the Amazon rain forest

They were tree farming, say some scientists who have investigated sites in Amazonia. According to this theory, the early inhabitants laboriously cleared tiny plots with their stone axes. Instead of planting crops that they could grow for a couple of years before the returning forest overwhelmed them, though, they planted trees that would provide food for a long, long time and would need little tending. Rather than cutting down the forest to make gardens, in other words, they replaced the natural forest with an artificial forest of useful trees.

Amazonia has no shortage of tree crops. There are fruit trees, nut trees, palm trees with edible parts, even a tree that produces a vanilla-flavored fruit called the ice-cream bean. Of the region's 138 known species of domesticated plants, more than half are trees. "Visitors are always amazed that you can walk in the forest here and constantly pick fruit from trees," says Charles R. Clement, an expert on plants. "That's because people *planted* them. They're walking through old orchards."

SECRETS OF PAINTED ROCK CAVE

The city of Santarém sits on the south bank of the Amazon River in Brazil. Across the river, sandstone buttes rise to heights of 500 feet and more, an unusual sight in the flat world of Amazonia. Caves in the buttes show signs of human activity. Their walls are splattered with ancient rock paintings: pictures of hands, stars, frogs, and human figures. One of these caves, Painted Rock Cave, was excavated in the 1990s by an archaeologist named Anna C. Roosevelt. She and her colleagues at first found evidence that Paleoindians lived in the cave as long ago as 6000 BC. The Paleoindians had pottery bowls—the oldest known pottery in the Americas. Roosevelt called those ancient people the Paituna culture, after a nearby village.

Roosevelt kept digging, though, and then she found something completely unexpected: a deeper, much older, layer of human habitation. According to this evidence, Paleoindians lived in Painted Rock Cave, ate fruit and fish, and left painted handprints on the wall almost 13,000 years ago, while the Clovis people were hunting bison in North America. Human history in Amazonia goes back a long way.

Clement studies how people have used plants in Brazil. He and some other experts have come to think that much of the Amazon forest—maybe all of it except the parts that flood every year during the rainy season—was created by humans. Over thousands of years, by planting a few trees here and a few trees there, the Amazonians slowly turned the river basin into a landscape that nourished human life. That landscape still reflects the guiding hand of generations of orchard planters.

Traces of ancient Indian handiwork can also be seen in the Beni, a vast plain in eastern Bolivia. The Beni lies on the southern edge of the Amazon basin and is about as large as the states of Indiana and Illinois combined. For half of each year, the Beni floods with water that flows down from melted snow in the Andes Mountains. The rest of the time, the Beni is almost as dry as a desert.

As many as 10,000 islands of forest dot the Beni. Each of these mounds rises as much as 60 feet above the surrounding plain. Trees that would die in the annual floods can grow on the islands, which are linked by long, straight raised mounds like elevated roadways.

Some archaeologists think that the forest islands of the Beni and other similar places in and around Amazonia were built by large, well-organized Indian societies many years before Columbus came ashore in the Americas. People built the islands so that they and their trees could survive the yearly floods.

If these archaeologists are right, tropical South America was home to highly developed cultures that skillfully engineered their environments. These cultures collapsed or faded away after the Europeans arrived, leaving only earthworks and other hard-to-recognize traces. Is this view of ancient Amazonia true? Only further research will tell. One area of research does not concern the landscape of Amazonia but rather the ground itself.

BLACK EARTH

Terra preta do Índio, people call it in Brazil—"black Indian Earth." Although the soil of Amazonia is generally poor, there are many patches of good soil. This good soil is fertile and rich in nutrients. Despite the Amazon's punishing rain and sun, it can produce crops for many years with little or no fertilizer. This *terra preta*, or black earth, is often found on low bluffs or hills at the edge of the floodplain, the area covered by water in the rainy season. The terra preta usually forms a layer one or two feet deep, but can be as much as six feet deep.

What caused this unusual soil to form at these locations? The clue lies in what the soil often contains—many small pieces of broken pottery. Scientists believe that the black earth did not occur naturally but was created by the same people who made the pottery.

Pottery pieces don't give black earth its remarkable and long-lasting fertility. The soil's power lies in charcoal—plant matter burned at a low temperature—which binds nutrients in the soil. Burning trees completely in slash-and-burn agriculture doesn't produce nearly enough charcoal to make black earth. Instead, the Indians had to practice "slash-and-char." They burned the plant matter only partway, creating charcoal, then stirred it into the soil. (Indians in some parts of South America still treat the soil this way today.) Black earth was also enriched with other organic substances, including human feces, kitchen waste, and the bones of turtles and fish. Special microorganisms such as bacteria that live in this soil may also enrich it and help keep it fertile for a long time.

Scientists from Brazil and the United States are still mapping the locations of terra preta in Amazonia. They are also studying the history and properties of this human-made soil. Their research may do more than reveal the skill of Amazonia's ancient soil-crafters. Perhaps methods of creating black earth will one day be used to rescue damaged or infertile land around the world.

Below: Brazilian Indian using a *zarabatana*, or shooting tube, a hunting weapon

CHAPTER 10

LAND OF FIRE

A DUTCH LAWYER NAMED ADRIAEN VAN DER DONCK LIVED AND worked in the Hudson River Valley in the 1640s, when European settlement in North America was still fairly new. Whenever he could, van der Donck ignored his duties and went off tramping around the forests and valleys of what is now upstate New York. He spent a lot of time with the local Native Americans, who called themselves the Haudenosaunee, although European histories usually refer to them as the Iroquois.

Later, during a five-year stay in Europe, van der Donck longed to be back in America. He wrote lovingly of his life there. Each fall, he said, was marked by huge blazes, when the Haudenosaunee set fire to the fields and forests. At first, these wildfires had scared van der Donck, but he came to know why the Indians started them. If all the dead weeds, grass, and shrubs burned off, tender new growth would carpet the forest the following spring, attracting the deer the Haudenosaunee liked to hunt.

Over time, van der Donck had come to enjoy the spectacle of the yearly burning. "Such a fire is a splendid sight when one sails on the rivers at night while the forest is ablaze on both banks," he wrote. With the forest burning to the right and left, the colonists stared in wonder as their boats passed through a channel of fire. During the burning season, said van der Donck, fire and flames were seen everywhere, creating a "delightful scene to look upon from afar."

Opposite: Indians in the Hudson River Valley, 1609

The Grass Fire (1908), by the well-known painter Frederic Remington, showed native peoples using controlled brush fires to create tender new growth that later would attract game animals.

NEARLY EVERY INDIAN GROUP SHAPED ITS ENVIRONMENT, AT LEAST IN PART, BY FIRE.

Frederic Remington
1905

Below: Bison dance of the Mandan Indians in front of their medicine lodge

The Haudenosaunee of the Hudson River Valley were not the only Native Americans to burn their land. Across North America, from the Atlantic Ocean to the Pacific and from Hudson Bay in the north to the Río Grande in the south, Indians set woodlands and plains ablaze. Nearly every Indian group shaped its environment, at least in part, by fire.

FLAME AND FOREST

When Native Americans put the landscape to the torch, they were deliberately interrupting a natural process that ecologists call succession. It is the series of stages that an ecosystem goes through as open land is filled. One of the clearest examples of succession in modern times is happening right now in southern Washington state, where a volcano named Mount St. Helens erupted violently in 1980.

Before the eruption, the mountain slopes were covered with dense, mature forest. The eruption buried more than 200 square miles in rock, ash, and mud, uprooting tens of thousands of trees. Within weeks, though, the devastated area was springing back to life. Lupines and other weeds and wildflowers were the first to take root in the burned-over soil. They prepared the ground for the return of the grasses.

Fifteen years after the eruption, the ravaged slopes were dotted with trees and woody shrubs, such as lodgepole pine and willow bush. Forest giants such as hemlock, Douglas fir, and Sitka spruce will be the next to move in. Each set of plants succeeds, or follows, the one ahead of it, until the ecosystem reaches its final stage, the tall forest.

If ecological succession never stopped, the continents would be covered with final-stage vegetation. We would live in a world of great trees, dark and silent. Weeds, grasses, brush, and shrubs would be uncommon. Succession is interrupted all the time, however. Sometimes, the interruption is a huge event like the eruption of Mount St. Helens, which clears a large area where succession can start over again from the beginning. Sometimes the interruption is much smaller. A windstorm may blow down two or three trees, creating a small clearing in the middle of a forest. Floodwaters may sweep a meadow clear of shrubs, letting the grasses flourish again. For the past 10,000 years, though, the most important force on North American ecosystems has been fire.

Fire resets the ecological clock. After a fire, the plants in an ecosystem (and the animals that depend on the plants for food and shelter) go back a few stages in the order of succession. A forest fire is a boost to plants and animals that need open sky and sunlight, a setback to those that love the cool shade of the forest floor. Different groups of plants and animals rise and fall over time as fire reshapes the landscape, and the cycle of succession repeats itself.

CONTROLLED BURNING

Fire has two main sources: lightning and people. In North America, lightning fire is most common in the western mountains. In other places, in the past, Indians controlled fire. They carried flints, hard stones that they struck together to create sparks and light their torches. When you think of Indians hunting, you probably picture them using bows and arrows. Torches, though, were just as important.

Native Americans used flame to chase down all kinds of game: deer in the Northeast, alligators in the Everglades, buffalo on the Great Plains, edible grasshoppers in the deserts of Utah and Nevada, rabbits in California, and moose in Alaska. Thomas Jefferson described how the Indians used fire in the hunt. They made big rings of flame by setting fire to fallen leaves. Heat and flame gradually forced the animals to the center of the ring, where the Indians could slaughter them with arrows, darts, and spears.

"THE SIGHT IS GRAND AND AWFUL"

In late 1792, Peter Fidler rode out with several groups of Indians across the plains of southern Alberta, Canada. Fidler was the first European to make a careful survey of that area. "Grass all burnt this day," he reported on November 12. "Not a single pine to be seen three days past." The next day, he reported that the land was burned, and the next. A month later, Fidler reported that the grass was burning "with very great fury."

"Every fall & spring," wrote Fidler, "& even in the winter when there is no snow, these large plains either in one place or another is constantly on fire, & when the Grass happens to be long & the wind high, the sight is grand & awful, & it drives along with amazing swiftness."

Prairie fires could be dangerous, but Fidler understood their purpose. The burning of the old grass, he knew, meant that the next spring and summer would bring fresh new grass—"excellent fine sweet feed for the Horses & Buffalo." In his ride across the Canadian plains, Fidler witnessed the ancient Native American art of landscaping by fire.

Native Americans also engineered their ecosystems to support game animals such as deer, elk, and bear. By constantly burning the undergrowth, they encouraged a rich new growth of grasses, bushes, and other early stage vegetation that fed large numbers of plant-eating animals. This, in turn, supported predators that fed on the plant eaters, and people who ate both plant eaters and predators. This controlled burning insured a steady supply of meat.

Henry David Thoreau, an American writer of the nineteenth century, imagined how eastern North America must have looked centuries before the Europeans arrived. He thought it must have been a monumental, unbroken forest, a dense wilderness of old trees. Thoreau was wrong. The eastern forest was an ecological patchwork of garden plots, fields of blackberries, open meadowlands or grassy areas, and forest.

Bison or buffalo now graze on the plains west of the Mississippi River. When the first colonists arrived in eastern North America, though, bison roamed from New York to Georgia, far outside their original range. These animals had been drawn east by the Native Americans, who used fire to turn large paths of forest into grassland or meadow, creating habitat for the herds. The Indians who hunted bison in the east were harvesting a food source that they had helped create.

Indian fire had its biggest impact in the middle of the continent. Native Americans turned the center of North America into a vast game farm. They burned the Great Plains and the Midwest prairies so much and so often that they made them bigger. When explorers Meriwether Lewis and William Clark headed west from the Mississippi River across the giant grassland in 1804, they were not crossing a wilderness. They were crossing a huge pasture that Native Americans had managed for thousands of years.

Carrying their flints and their torches, the Indians lived in balance with nature, but it was a balance that they constantly adjusted. They had shaped the American landscape until it fit their lives like comfortable clothing. The Native American system of land management worked for a long, long time—but by the time the Europeans arrived, some Indians were abandoning it. They had taken up a different way of life, one that changed the way they related to the landscape.

THE MOUND BUILDERS

Anyone who traveled up the Mississippi River 900 years ago would have seen, looming in the distance, a four-level mound of earth, built by human hands, that was bigger than Egypt's Great Pyramid. Around this huge mound stood more than a hundred smaller mounds, some topped with walls of wooden poles. Canals for irrigation and transportation threaded among fields of maize. Wooden houses were covered with red and white plaster. Flags of painted animal skin flapped everywhere. This splendid sight was Cahokia, home to at least 15,000 Native Americans.

Cahokia stood near the present-day site of St. Louis, Missouri. In the eighteenth century, it was the largest settlement north of the Río Grande, and it was also part of a long tradition of mound building in the eastern half of North America. Over thousands of years, societies along the Mississippi and the rivers that flowed into it, and some in the Southeast, constructed tens of thousands of mounds across the land.

Most mounds were shaped like giant cones or layered pyramids. Some, though, were sculpted into enormous birds, lizards, bears, or long-tailed creatures such as alligators. Near Peebles, Ohio, is a 1,300-foot long mound in the shape of a snake.

Mound Builders, 3400 BC – AD 1400

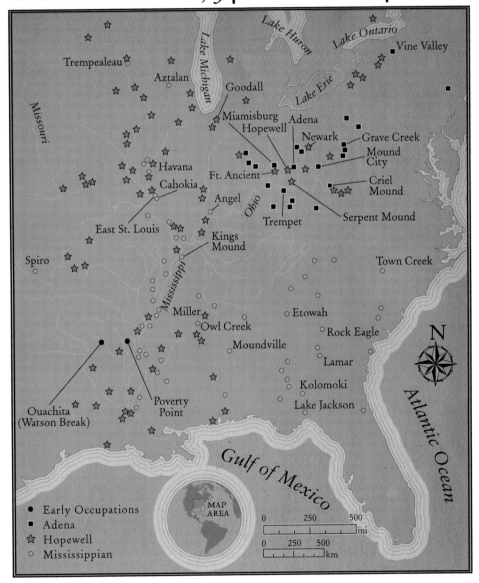

- ● Early Occupations
- ■ Adena
- ☆ Hopewell
- ○ Mississippian

Some societies used the mounds as tombs, burying their nobles inside with textiles, tools, and jewelry.

The earliest known mounds are in Louisiana and are about 5,400 years old. The majority were built later, between 3400 BC and AD 1400. Because mound building is a long-term activity that requires some kind of organization and authority, it tells us that some early Indians lived in settled communities instead of roving in small hunting bands. No one knows exactly why these communities built the mounds, but the structures probably served religious purposes. Some societies used them as tombs, burying their nobles inside the mounds with textiles, tools, and jewelry.

Archaeologists don't know what the societies who built the mounds called themselves, but they have given names to several distinct cultures. The Adena culture, which flourished from about 800 to 100 BC, started something big—agriculture. The Adena domesticated a variety of edible or useful native plants, including knotweed, maygrass, and tobacco.

The Hopewell culture followed the Adena. Hopewell people developed a wide-ranging trade network that exchanged goods such as silver from Ontario, in Canada, and seashells from the Gulf of Mexico. They continued to build mounds and to farm as the Adena had done. Later, after the Hopewell culture declined, the Mississippian culture arose in the Southeast and along the southern Mississippi River. Cahokia was one piece in the patchwork of Mississippian chiefdoms, but it was a big piece.

THE RISE AND FALL OF CAHOKIA

Cahokia's golden age lasted from about AD 950 to 1250. Its people weren't typical urban dwellers, such as merchants or specialized crafts workers. Cahokia was a lot of farmers living very close together. It started out as a cluster of small villages but grew rapidly when people moved to the area to take part in the great mound building project. The city of mounds was made possible by an agricultural revolution—the shift to growing maize.

Left: The Indian Serpent Mound in southern Ohio was apparently built around AD 1050, though some archaeologists believe it is even older.

Above: Cahokia as it may have looked at the city's peak

Before Cahokia's rise, people were slowly hunting the local deer and bison toward extinction. Meat was becoming scarcer, and farming couldn't make up the difference. Most crops, such as maygrass, had tiny seeds. It took a huge amount of seeds (and work) to feed a family. The people needed a new food source, and they found one.

Although maize had been around for hundreds of years, the Hopewell people hadn't shown much interest in it. Around AD 800, though, the hungry Mississippians started cultivating maize in the flat plains along the river. Maize fed the growing population of the area, and it also fed the growth of community institutions, such as storehouses for grain. Organizing and supervising the building of storehouses is one way a central power could have emerged. From there it was a short step to building other community structures, such as the mounds and canals.

Although maize helped Cahokia rise, it also played a part in the city's downfall. Cahokia was the first time Indians north of the Río Grande had tried to feed and shelter 15,000 people in one place, and they made beginner's mistakes. To get wood

The American Bottom, AD 1300

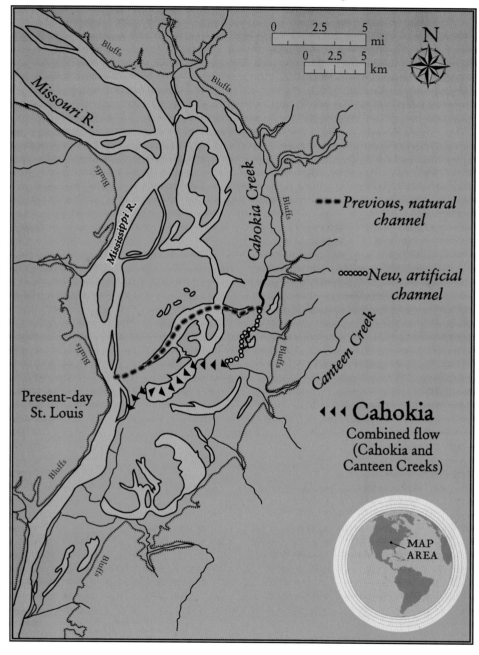

- - - *Previous, natural channel*

ooooooo *New, artificial channel*

◄◄◄ **Cahokia**
Combined flow
(Cahokia and
Canteen Creeks)

MAP AREA

for cooking-fires and home construction, they cut all the trees on the surrounding hills. To clear fields for maize, they removed all the brush and natural vegetation. Because the city kept getting bigger, the brush and forest could not return.

Meanwhile, people went farther and farther out to cut trees. Hauling the logs back to the city became more and more difficult. Sometime between AD 1100 and 1200, the Cahokians dug a long channel that caused part of a second, larger creek to dump its water into Canteen Creek. This turned Canteen Creek into a river flowing right through the city. Woodcutters upstream could float logs down to Cahokia on the new waterway, which also provided the city with plenty of water.

Too much water, it turned out. Heavy summer rains beat down on the area. Without trees on the hills to slow the flow of water, rainfall rushed rapidly into the creeks, making them deeper and faster than ever. Mudslides and floods became common. Starting about 1200, Canteen Creek flooded again and again, destroying Cahokia's maize harvests. Then, sometime around 1300, a big earthquake struck. Already weakened by the floods, the city never recovered. There was social unrest, maybe even civil war. By 1350, the city was almost empty.

A CHANGING LANDSCAPE

While the Cahokians were planting their fields and building their mounds, maize was spreading through the eastern half of what is now the United States. For thousands of years, Native Americans had shaped the landscape mainly with fire. They used their axes only to clear small gardens. As maize swept in, though, Indians burned and chopped thousands of acres, mainly in river valleys, to plant the new crop, and they kept the new fields clear. After a period of trial and error, they learned how to plant wisely, to avoid floods and mudslides. Before long, maize fields surrounded many villages.

Forest surrounded the fields, but the Indians were changing the forest, too. Before, they had burned the undergrowth to create new growth for grazing deer and elk. Now they started replanting large stretches of woodland, turning them into orchards of fruit and nut trees. They harvested chestnuts, hickory nuts, hazelnuts, beechnuts, acorns, pecans, walnuts, and butternuts from thousands of trees that they had planted.

Within a few hundred years after adopting maize, the Indians of the eastern forest had transformed their landscape. What was once a patchwork game park had become a mixture of farmland and orchards. Enough forest was left to allow for hunting, but agriculture was on the rise. The Native Americans had created a new balance of nature.

Within a few
hundred years,
the Indians
had transformed
their landscape.

CHAPTER 11

THE CREATED WILDERNESS

PILGRIMS AND OTHER EARLY SETTLERS IN NORTH AMERICA ARE OFTEN described as finding themselves on the edge of a vast natural wilderness. In reality, they arrived in a land that had been cultivated by humans for a long time. Native Americans had shaped the land through fire, farming, and tree planting to suit their own purposes, but the Pilgrims' arrival coincided with waves of diseases that were killing the Native Americans. The deaths of the people who shaped the landscape made the land return to an untamed state. Then, when the Pilgrims and other Europeans settled the land, they thought that was how it had always been—a wilderness.

The smallpox epidemic that swept through Tenochtitlán at the time of Cortés's attack was an early sign of what was to come. So was the devastation from disease in Peru at the time of Pizarro's conquest. Far to the north, just before the Pilgrims arrived, an Indian named Tisquantum witnessed the same kind of destruction.

TISQUANTUM'S HOMECOMING

Tisquantum, known to generations of American schoolchildren as Squanto, was a member of the Wampanoag people of New England. He grew up in Patuxet, a village on Cape Cod Bay. In 1614 he was kidnapped by Thomas Hunt, the captain of an English ship that visited the coast.

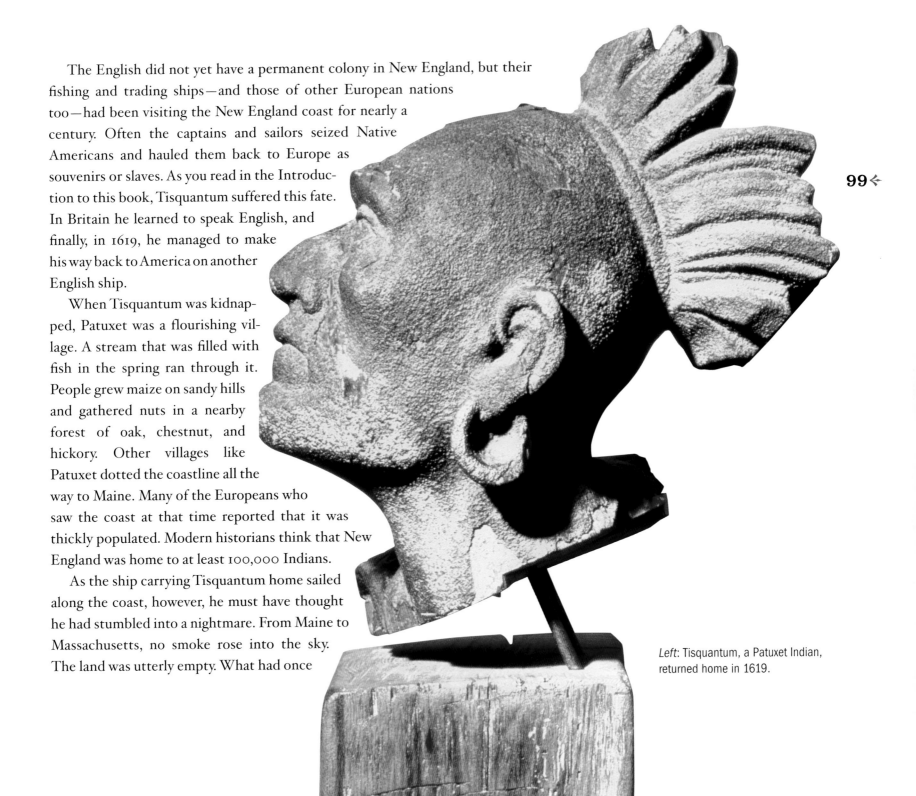

The English did not yet have a permanent colony in New England, but their fishing and trading ships—and those of other European nations too—had been visiting the New England coast for nearly a century. Often the captains and sailors seized Native Americans and hauled them back to Europe as souvenirs or slaves. As you read in the Introduction to this book, Tisquantum suffered this fate. In Britain he learned to speak English, and finally, in 1619, he managed to make his way back to America on another English ship.

When Tisquantum was kidnapped, Patuxet was a flourishing village. A stream that was filled with fish in the spring ran through it. People grew maize on sandy hills and gathered nuts in a nearby forest of oak, chestnut, and hickory. Other villages like Patuxet dotted the coastline all the way to Maine. Many of the Europeans who saw the coast at that time reported that it was thickly populated. Modern historians think that New England was home to at least 100,000 Indians.

As the ship carrying Tisquantum home sailed along the coast, however, he must have thought he had stumbled into a nightmare. From Maine to Massachusetts, no smoke rose into the sky. The land was utterly empty. What had once

Left: Tisquantum, a Patuxet Indian, returned home in 1619.

Below: The Pilgrims discovering stores of Indian corn

been a line of busy communities was now a mass of tumbledown homes and untended fields. Scattered among the houses and fields were human skeletons, bleached white by the sun. The whole coast had become a cemetery.

Patuxet had been hit hard. No one there remained alive. Tisquantum and his English companions marched inland, passing settlements that lay quiet and empty, full of the dead. Finally they found some survivors in a shattered village, and Tisquantum learned what had happened.

In 1616, a French ship was wrecked on Cape Cod, and the Indians took some of the sailors prisoner. The sailors carried a disease, though, and their Indian captors caught it. More Indians became ill, and still more. By 1619, the disease had killed 90 percent of the Native Americans of New England. Some modern researchers think this particular epidemic was a form of hepatitis, perhaps spread by contaminated food.

Tisquantum had finally returned home, only to find that in just a few years, his family, his friends, his village—his entire social world—had disappeared. Stunned, he returned with his English companions to their ship and sailed with them to Maine. Once he got there, however, Tisquantum realized he could not stay. He had to go back to Massachusetts. On his journey back, some surviving Wampanoag took him prisoner, probably because he was linked to the hated Europeans, kidnappers and bringers of disease.

By 1619, disease had killed 90 percent of the Native Americans of New England.

THE SMALLPOX
EPIDEMIC
PICKED OFF VICTIMS LIKE A SNIPER—
10 TO 30 A DAY.

THE FRIENDLY INDIAN

Soon afterward, the English settlers called Pilgrims arrived to establish a colony at Plymouth Bay, in Massachusetts. The Pilgrims found the land nearly empty of inhabitants. Desperate for food, they ransacked abandoned Indian houses for their stores of grain. Some Native Americans in the area were still alive, and the Pilgrims were able to communicate with them through Tisquantum.

Tisquantum would go down in history as the "friendly Indian" who came to help the Pilgrims. In reality, he was sent to them by Massasoit, the Wampanoag leader. Massasoit mistrusted Tisquantum, but he didn't like or trust the Pilgrims, either. He thought they might be useful allies against another neighboring Indian group, the Narragansett, however. The Narragansett hadn't been hit by the plague, and now they greatly outnumbered the Wampanoag. Massasoit wanted to get the Pilgrims on his side in case of trouble with the Narrangansett. Once Massasoit had decided to make contact with the Pilgrims, he had no choice but to use Tisquantum, the only available translator.

The Pilgrims' governor, Edward Winslow, who succeeded William Bradford as governor, wrote that one of the ways in which Tisquantum helped was by teaching the English settlers to plant corn. His method included burying fish alongside the maize seeds to fertilize the soil and produce a good harvest. This may not be a traditional Indian farming tip, however. Researchers have found little evidence that Native Americans planted fish with their maize. Farmers in parts of Europe, however, had used fish as

Below: The Pilgrims receiving Massasoit

fertilizer for hundreds of years. During his travels in Europe, Tisquantum had stayed in places where people planted fish with their crops. He may have learned about fish-fertilizer in Europe and then introduced it to the Pilgrims, and to other Indians as well.

Wherever the fish-fertilizer idea came from, the Pilgrims were lucky to have Tisquantum's help. They were lucky in other ways too. They might not have survived that first hungry winter without the maize left behind by Indians who had died. In addition, they might not have been able to plant a lasting settlement on the coast if the Indians hadn't been removed by disease . . . a disease brought by earlier European visitors.

WAVES OF DISEASE

As happened in Mexico and Peru, North America was struck by epidemics of contagious disease as soon as they began contact with Europeans. Disease didn't die away after just one or two outbreaks, however. Epidemics kept happening throughout the colonial period.

Two of the worst outbreaks of smallpox struck just before and during the Revolutionary War. These epidemics didn't just kill Native Americans; they killed colonists, too. By this time, the colonies contained a lot of people who had been born in America. Because smallpox was only an occasional, terrible visitor, however, many colonists born in the Americas had never been exposed to it. Like the Indians, they had not acquired childhood immunity.

The first smallpox epidemic started outside Boston in 1774. It lurked in the area for several years, picking off victims like a sniper—10 to 30 a day. John Adams of Massachusetts, one of the leaders of the Revolution, wrote to his wife, "The small Pox! The small Pox! What shall We do with it?" So many revolutionary fighters died of smallpox that Adams and others feared that the disease, not British soldiers, would crush the American rebellion.

Smallpox spread among Native Americans up and down the coast. It attacked the

The epidemic spread all the way to the Pacific coast.

Tsalagi and the Haudenosaunee, known to Europeans as the Cherokee and the Iroquois leagues. Both groups were allies of the British, but after the epidemic, they were too weak to fight well—so the epidemic helped the revolutionaries as well as hurt them.

In 1779, as the epidemic faded along the Atlantic coast, smallpox broke out in Spain's Mexico colony. It raged through Mexico City, killing as many as 18,000 in less than half a year, then tore south through Central America.

This epidemic also traveled north. In 1780, people started dying of smallpox along the road to Santa Fe, New Mexico. From there, the disease exploded into a completely new territory: western North America. Traveling along Native American trade routes that had hummed with activity since ancient times, smallpox reached the shore of Hudson Bay, in northern Canada, in two years.

Just before dawn one day in 1781, a group of Blackfoot Indians came across a Shoshone camp in Alberta, Canada. Because the two groups were rivals, the Blackfoot attacked the sleeping Shoshone. When they sliced open the Shoshone tents and went in to fight, though, they halted in terror. One of them later said that "there was no one to fight with but the dead and dying." The Shoshone were covered with the telltale sores of smallpox. The Blackfoot didn't touch the bodies, but they got sick anyway.

The epidemic spread all the way to the Pacific coast. When a British explorer named George Vancouver visited Washington's Puget Sound in 1792, he found deserted villages, abandoned boats, and bodies scattered everywhere. The few survivors were scarred and blinded by smallpox.

A GARDEN WITHOUT GARDENERS

Across North America, the new diseases destroyed or weakened Native American societies. For centuries, these societies had managed the land—burning undergrowth each year, hunting bison and netting salmon, clearing and replanting forests, building canals and terraces and irrigation ditches, planting milpa and fields. When the Indians started to disappear, their managed environment suddenly became a garden without gardeners.

Without Indian fire to hold it back, forest started to spread into grasslands in places like Ohio, Missouri, and Texas. Everywhere, untended maize fields were overgrown with weeds, then bushes and trees. In the eastern forest, the open, parklike landscapes of groves and orchards quickly filled in, becoming dark, thick woods.

The animal life of the continent exploded too. With fewer Indians hunting them, deer, elk, and bison increased greatly in numbers. Game overran the land. In 1579, when Sir Francis Drake became the first English mariner to sail into San Francisco Bay, he saw a land of plenty, where uncountable numbers of large, fat deer roamed. Drake did not know that just a century earlier, before disease spread into California from places that had had contact with Europeans, the shoreline of the bay was thickly settled by Indians, and deer were much scarcer.

Bison might have suddenly become more numerous, too. When Hernando de Soto's expedition crisscrossed the Southeast for four years in the middle of the sixteenth century, the Spanish encountered many people, but their reports of the trip don't mention bison. When French explorers traveled down the Mississippi more than a century later, they found the land empty of people, although large bison herds grazed on the prairies along the river. For many people, these vast herds of bison are symbols of "natural" North America before

THE PASSING OF THE GREAT FLOCKS

"Blue meteors," some people called them. Passenger pigeons were bluish-gray in color and so swift in flight that they seemed to whiz across the sky like shooting stars. On the ground, these graceful birds became greedy gobblers, devouring seeds, nuts, fruit, and cereal grains. They could strip a field clean in minutes.

Enormous flocks of passenger pigeons flew over North America in the early years of European settlement. The flocks contained millions of birds—the sky was darkened for

Above: Hunters shooting into a huge flock of migrating passenger pigeons, 1875

minutes at a time when they passed overheard. During the eighteenth century, Indians and colonists alike hunted and ate the pigeons in great numbers. The hunt continued into the nineteenth century. Then, suddenly, the huge flocks were gone. The last known passenger pigeon was named Martha after George Washington's wife. When Martha died in 1914, the species became extinct.

Passenger pigeons are sometimes called symbols of the great natural abundance of wildlife in America before European settlement brought guns and began to overhunt. They are also symbols of how people can carelessly and recklessly destroy a natural resource. Some researchers, though, believe that the immense flocks of passenger pigeons were unknown before Columbus came to the Americas. Passenger pigeons did exist, but not in such extraordinary numbers.

Six surveys of bones at Cahokia, where Native Americans lived for hundreds of years, showed what the people ate. The surveys found lots of bones from animals, birds, and even fish, but only a few passenger pigeon bones. William I. Woods, who has studied Cahokia for many years, thinks that in the centuries before Columbus, the passenger pigeon was not particularly common. After disease started killing the Native Americans who had tended the land, however, their abandoned fields, gardens, and orchards were suddenly available as a food source for the passenger pigeon, and the pigeon's numbers went sharply up. The huge historic flocks of passenger pigeons, in this theory, were created only after European diseases had ended the Indians' long management of their environment.

the Europeans came. Some researchers now think, though, that the herds became huge only after the new diseases started killing Indian hunters.

There are many ways to peer into the past. Archaeologists who are examining places where Native Americans lived can count the bones and seeds in their old garbage pits to learn what they ate. Environmental scientists can study how people, plants, and animals interact to learn how changing one species affects the other species that share its ecosystem. In these and many other ways, archaeologists and ecologists are revealing a new picture of the American past.

Much remains to be learned about the details, and not all experts agree on all points. Still, most researchers now agree that the Native Americans managed their ecosystems on a large scale. When the Indians suddenly lost massive numbers of people to disease, they could no longer manage their ecosystems on that scale, and things started to change.

It happened fast. Many of the first European explorers and settlers in the Americas wrote about finding abandoned fields and forest groves that were so free of undergrowth that they could gallop through them on horses, or ride among the trees in carriages. This was a landscape that had been created by the Native Americans. Already, though, the forest was taking over.

By the time of the American Revolution in the late eighteenth century, many parts of the continent were covered with thick, uninhabited woodland. The people of the newly created United States did not realize that much of the land had been very different when the first Europeans arrived. They thought that the forest had been there forever, primitive and unchanging.

The forest was just the latest transformation of the landscape, however. Change began with the Native American peoples, who manipulated their environment for thousands of years. When they were no longer around to oversee their parklands, woodlands, orchards, and gardens, the forest took over. Human beings had shaped the landscape, and human beings and their diseases helped create the wilderness that followed.

Below: Landing of Columbus

It may be a while before our schoolbooks and TV shows catch up with the fact that the Americas were not a wilderness when the European settlers arrived, or that the forests of Amazonia contain thousands of carefully planted tree gardens, or that pyramids existed on the coast of Peru before they existed in Egypt. These and other revolutionary new views of the past are still taking shape, as fresh discoveries and discussions add to our knowledge of the Americas before Columbus.

Early Native American societies were older, bigger, and more complex than modern historians once thought. For thousands of years, as they created maize, landscaped with fire, and managed populations of game animals, Indians made use of the land. They also built cultures whose influence remains strong in millions of lives today, from the Arctic through South America.

The arrival of Europeans and their diseases plunged Native Americans into a long decline, but in the early twenty-first century the Indians' numbers have begun to rise. Just as Indians interacted with the landscape of the Americas in the past, they will play a part in deciding what it will look like, and how it will be used, in the future.

GLOSSARY

altiplano: The landscape of high plains between the twin ranges of the Andes Mountains

Andean: Related to the Andes Mountains of western South America

archaeology: The study of earlier people and civilizations, usually through examining the ruins of their buildings and other objects they left behind

artifact: A human-made object, such as a tool, weapon, or work of art

Beringia: The name modern scientists have given to the bridge of dry land that connected Siberia with Alaska during the ice ages, when the ocean level was much lower than it is now

conquistador: Spanish soldier-adventurer involved in the exploration and conquest of the Americas; the word means "conqueror"

geology: The study of the earth, the rocks of which it is made, and their changes over time

glyph: Symbol that the ancient Mesoamerican peoples used in writing

HLA profile: The arrangement of HLAs (disease-fighting molecules called human leukocyte antigens) that each person inherits from his or her parents

maize: Corn

megafauna: Large animals

Mesoamerica: The region that includes Mexico and Central America

milpa: The traditional Mesoamerican field or garden plot, in which farms grow both maize and beans, together with a variety of other crops, such as squash, peppers, and avocados

Paleoindians: The earliest inhabitants of the Americas, before modern Native American cutures appeared; *paleo* means "old"

paleontology: The study of ancient or extinct plants and animals, usually through fossils

Pleistocene epoch: A period of prehistoric time that ended about 10,000 years ago

radiocarbon dating: A method used by archaeologists to tell the age of anything that was once alive, such as bones, charcoal from burned wood, or leather; it works by measuring the decay of carbon atoms found in all living things

stratigraphy: A key principle of archaeology that says that the age of a fossil or artifact is related to where it is found among the strata, or layers, of the earth; in general, deeper strata are older than the strata that lie above them

swidden farming: Also called slash-and-burn agriculture; a method of farming in which people cut down the trees and brush on a small field, burn the vegetation to enrich the soil with nitrogen, farm for a few years until the soil loses its fertility, and then move on to another plot

zoonotic disease: A disease, such as influenza or smallpox, that originates in animals and travels to humans

FURTHER READING

Baquedano, Elizabeth, and Barry Clarke. *Aztec, Inca, and Maya*. New York: DK Publishing, Inc., 2005.

Calloway, Colin G. *One Vast Winter Count: The Native American West Before Lewis and Clark*. Lincoln: University of Nebraska Press, 2003.

Calvert, Patricia. *The Ancient Inca*. New York: Franklin Watts, 2004.

Cooke, Tim. *Ancient Aztec: Archaeology Unlocks the Secrets of Mexico's Past*. Washington, DC: National Geographic Society, 2007.

Fleet, Cameron, ed. *First Nations—Firsthand: A History of Five Hundred Years of Encounter, War, and Peace Inspired by the Eyewitnesses*. Edison, NJ: Chartwell Books, 1997.

Hakim, Joy. *First Americans*. New York: Oxford University Press, 2005.

Josephy, Alvin M., Jr. *500 Nations: An Illustrated History of North American Indians*. New York: Gramercy Books, 2002.

McCall, Barbara. *Native American Culture: The European Invasion*. Vero Beach, FL: Rourke Publications, Inc., 1994.

Nicholson, Sue. *Aztecs and Incas: A Guide to the Pre-Colonized Americas in 1504*. London: Kingfisher, 2000.

Page, Jake. *In the Hands of the Great Spirit: The 20,000-Year History of American Indians*. New York: Free Press, 2003.

Thomas, David Hurst, et al. *Native Americans: An Illustrated History*. Atlanta: Turner Publishing, Inc., 1993.

Wilson, James. *The Earth Shall Weep: A History of Native America*. New York: Atlantic Monthly Press, 1999.

Wright, Ronald. *Stolen Continents: Five Hundred Years of Conquest and Resistance in the Americas*. Boston: Houghton Mifflin, 1992.

WEBSITES

Native American Cultures Canyon Rock Art
http://teacher.scholastic.com/activities/explorer/native_americans/mission_canyon.asp

Native American Homes
http://www.native-languages.org/houses.htm

National Museum of the American Indian
http://www.nmai.si.edu/exhibitions/first_american_art/firstamericanart.html

Carnegie Museum of Natural History
http://www.carnegiemnh.org/exhibits/north-south-east-west

PHOTO AND ILLUSTRATION CREDITS

INDEX

116